THY SUN, THY ROD, AND THY STAFF

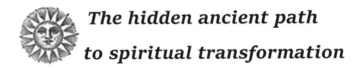

The hidden ancient path to spiritual transformation

Michael Erevna

Thy Sun, Thy Rod, & Thy Staff, by Michael Erevna, Published by Amazon Kindle Direct Publishing with RevelationNow.net

Cover by Michael Erevna.

Paperback ISBN: 978-1-64370-397-8
Paperback ASIN: 1643703978

This book is not intended to be a substitute for the medical advice of a licensed physician. The reader should consult with their doctor in any matters relating to his/her health. Before beginning any new exercise program, fasting, or Sungazing, I recommend that you seek medical advice from your physician.

All images are for educational purposes.

Dedication

To my beloved, Marisol, the greatest love, and joy a person could ever wish. She was a wonderful wife, mother, and soul who encouraged me to start writing and sharing knowledge. You will be forever missed and always in my heart. This book is a product of your love, support, and spiritual steadfastness.

In loving memory of Marisol McLeod
(Dec. 4, 1971–Nov. 18, 2015)

My message and my preaching were not with wise and persuasive words, but with a demonstration of the Spirit's power,

1 Corinthians 2:4

Table of Contents

Acknowledgments

First, thanks to my parents for making me read so much at a young age! This book is a culmination of efforts from friends, family, and colleagues encouraging me with support. This book was a journey through a web of ancient artifacts, narratives, and ideas. I was fortunate to have studied the life of Jesus and juxtaposed remarkable similarities with ancient characters deemed, gods. I would be remiss if I did not mention the support from Tiana Worthy, Howard Moon, Terry Royster, Jamil Blackmon, and Alicia Harris during the writing process. I would like to express my gratitude to all of them for their support. For all their efforts I assume some errors made their way into this book, and I take responsibility for them. Finally, I would like to thank the Most High for giving me the insight, intuition, strength, and dedication to finish this book.

Preface

In ancient times there were men and women perceived as gods. These men and women could do amazing things the common man could not. To that end, their human status elevates to that of a god. Even though science still can't seem to discover a body of a divine being whose DNA isn't human.

These ancient men and women that possessed supernatural power were in fact human. Over vast epochs, each Age, spiritual emissaries appeared to teach those with interest how to activate their Spiritual power. Many people like to debate if Mithra, Dionisius, Krishna, Horus, or even Jesus were real, but they miss the point of their examples. They all demonstrated amazing abilities locked inside humans.

What made them legendary was they knew the secrets of unlocking the Kingdom within, while in a human body. All of them were considered gods except for Jesus who was considered King of Kings and part of the Godhead. How can any of us speak for the hierarchy of the Heavenly Kingdom? In the very beginning of time, humanity had no secrets, and God walked with man.

There was a methodology for humanity to activate its spiritual body. Much like the caterpillar who knew when to sleep and awaken transformed into a butterfly. The closer history was to ancient times there are more accounts of individuals who manifested godlike powers. Our closest example is Jesus and His Disciples. They all demonstrated the power of the Spirit.

Part of the mission of Jesus was to teach and demonstrate how to unlock the Kingdom within. The enemy of humans at the time were the Pharisees, and Jesus despised them. Jesus called them "liars" and "vipers" because the Pharisees hid the "keys of knowledge" for spiritual transformation. The Pharisees kept men trapped in the material world.

The ancient men and women who were called gods and goddesses were humans who practiced the same spiritual transformation process as Jesus. I am not talking about the gods and goddesses who represented Creator Forces and Cosmic Elements, because there is a distinction. The ones who eventually died were human. The true God never dies so we should reevaluate naming conventions for gods and goddess. By doing so, we make their godlike capabilities attainable and in line with the teachings of Jesus.

If we look to the Disciples, they were able to cast out demons, heal the sick, speak in different languages, and raise the dead, etc. Presently, I am unaware of anyone on Earth demonstrating this power of the Spirit. Lucky for humanity the ancients left many secrets hidden in plain view. Why were so many ancient gods referred to as Sun gods?

That was the norm in ancient times, and there were many Sun gods. Most people are only aware of Greek Sun gods, but Sun gods were universal and included Africa, Australia, Ainu, Arabian, Aztec, Baltic, Basque, Brazilian, and finally Buddhist. I believe not everyone could make it through the spiritual transformation process. It is a strict purification regimen which includes (Zaidi, 2011) fasting for 40 days, among other key components.

One of the by-products of completing the spiritual transformation process was a spiritual morality in line with the Heavenly Kingdom. Jesus was a perfect example of this and promoted a message of love and acceptance, *without* sin. The ancients were aware of the condition of the heart, which must be purified to ascend to spiritual transformation. Revaluating ancient ways are the only way to reclaim our spiritual bodies.

Without understanding the ancient practices, we will continue to be slaves to the modern-day church system, which cannot demonstrate one thing a Disciple did. The Vatican are stewards of ancient spiritual knowledge, yet much of it is locked away underneath the Vatican. Some say for miles and miles! What makes the Vatican different from the Pharisees in this sense? Are they not hiding the "keys of knowledge" as well? Why would the Vatican keep humans spiritually nonactivated? I think the answer is clear and that is for control and wealth generation. International bankers surmise the wealth of the Vatican is around $1.6 billion.

If people were spiritually activated they would no longer value the Vatican and the cash cow of spiritual ignorance would be no more. The Vatican is not just wealthy, but it influences global politics. By hoarding, securing, and refusing to release ancient text guarantees the survival of the Vatican. The Vatican behavior is nothing more than honoring the law of self-preservation.

I believe when Jesus returns the Vatican will be one of the first things to go. Our best choice now is to pursue the secrets to spiritual actuation because this is the Vatican's biggest fear. We must study what our great Teacher left us and discover the secrets left by ancient demonstrators of Spirit power. Before turning the page make sure you are ready for this journey.

You will no longer see Christianity or the Holy Spirit in the same light.

State of Spiritual Affairs

Proverbs 25:2

It is the glory of God to conceal a thing but the honor of kings to search it out.

Why has it been 2,000 years since anyone on Earth has performed one Biblically authentic act demonstrated by Jesus or His Disciples? Jesus made a promise to His Disciples they would be able to demonstrate more Spiritual powers than He because His time was short on Earth. Jesus incarnated on the Earth to re-educate and demonstrate human spiritual abilities locked away inside us and hidden from the masses. There has been an omission of *key teachings* to break spiritual transformation, communication with the Heavenly Kingdom, and transfer ideological control to a modern-day Pharisee church system.

Furthermore, the Vatican Crusades eradicated teachings for activating our spiritual selves to control the people of the Earth. Omission happened long before any of the other modern-day churches broke away from the Vatican, and they too preach a half-truth. What other church system is more powerful than the Vatican?

They are the global stewards of ancient spiritual knowledge over vast centuries.

For us to unlock the keys to our spiritual abilities, we must return to ancient artifacts and narratives before the ferreting away of the keys of knowledge. If you jettison Biblical accounts from this investigation, you will find older ancient cultures own many of the original accounts the Bible speaks. In fact, there are too many to be a coincidence. The Sumerians have seven-tablets of Creation, a flood, and a messiah.

These ancient cultures left simplistic symbols with meanings that transcend time and need viewing in the proper context. As the scientific understanding of quantum physics, progressively matures, ancient Egyptian hieroglyphics take on new insights. The agendas of secret societies and secret orders have not tainted ancient artifacts like the carved stone symbol of the (Britannica, 2016) Sun god Ashur. The seizing of antiquated information by mystery orders was never imparted to the uninitiated. What these secret orders could not do was locate *all* the ancient artifacts peppered around the Earth.

This book will take you on a journey to rediscover what ancient cultures embodied in stone because they possessed the full potential of the human/spiritual being. These ancient cultures knew the recipe for the biochemical activation (What is DNA Activation?, 2013) of dormant DNA and how to consciously transition to spirit. Ancient cultures witnessed and interacted with the Heavenly Kingdom 8.611 light years away located in the (McClure, 2018) Orion Nebula. I believe ancient Egyptian testimony from, (Ogden Goelet (Translator), 2015) "The Book of the Dead," is a mistranslation as a sole fascination with dead things when it is also a narrative of interaction with spiritual life while living.

Ancient spiritual practices relied on the Sun as the catalyst for a spiritual transformation. One of the least emphasized statements by Jesus, in 1 Corinthians 2:4, *"My message and my preaching were not with wise and persuasive words, but with a **demonstration** of the Spirit's power."* Jesus was merely trying to show humans what our spiritual capabilities are in human form. There is a strict spiritual actuation methodology, which must be followed to accomplish spiritual ignition; and some are easier said than others are!

Anybody bastardizing the teachings of Jesus with political platforms or any other material subjects will never achieve what Jesus promised us we could do.

Jesus said to follow His ways and not any other character in the Bible. Have you noticed many people who claim to be "servants" of Jesus are experts on darkness? How can you ever learn the hidden path if you are focusing on the distractions of this world or the modus operandi of secret societies and magical orders?

There is a whole other spiritual universe out there teeming with spiritual life, and Jesus incarnated on Earth to demonstrate the human abilities for interacting with it. We have DNA driven dormant abilities locked inside us, and they were suppressed to keep us prisoners in the material world. That incessant feeling something is wrong, and a longing for something not perceived is the soul's call for a return to Spirit. If it not for these unsullied ancient artifacts illustrating: the *pineal gland*, *DNA*, and the *Sun;* subsequently trapping us in church doctrine. Why do we follow pastors and preachers who cannot demonstrate one act of Jesus or the Disciples?

Modern-day clergymen are Divinity students of spiritual teachings where there was a removal of key elements hundreds of years ago! Many of these pastors and preachers have the best spiritual intentions while most are just interested in enriching themselves off the hopes and naivety of people. Jesus and the Disciples demonstrated the Spirit's power for people to witnesses what He said they could do. Does it make sense to follow people who *cannot* demonstrate this power? Would you trust the teachings of an obese fitness trainer? Either you *know* the true hidden path, and you can demonstrate it, or you cannot!

Our collective consciousness should focus on ancient evidence and re-discover what is hidden. Modern man is unable to replicate many of the ancient wonders of the world because the ancients were receiving knowledge from the Spirit realm. We are hybrid beings made of flesh and spirit, yet our spiritual capabilities are dormant. This book will present ancient findings in a new way in the hopes of activating our spiritual selves.

Finally, Scripture like the 23rd Psalm contains clues that tell a greater story. In verse 4 of this Psalm, it says, "...*thy rod and thy staff they comfort me.*" How can a rod and staff comfort you? The rod and the staff must possess properties, which provide the human body with relief in some form.

There is another insight linked to the "rod and the staff," and this book finds the underlying cause of it, in the ancient past. These are mysteries the uninitiated will never understand, and there is an application of the "rod and the staff" that leads to peace. There is a direct connection to the 23rd Psalm and a process for spiritual transformation. The modern church system does not use the rod and the staff.

> Psalm 23 (KJV) - *23 The Lord is my shepherd; I shall not want. 2 He maketh me to lie down in green pastures: he leadeth me beside still waters. 3 He restoreth my soul: he leadeth me in the paths of righteousness for his name's sake. 4 Yea, though I walk through the valley of the shadow of death, I will fear no evil: for thou art with me;* **thy rod and thy staff they comfort me.** *5 Thou preparest a table before me in the presence of mine enemies: thou anointest my head with oil; my cup runneth over. 6 Surely goodness and mercy shall follow me all the days of my life: and I will dwell in the house of the Lord forever.*

There is an ancient practice for everything mentioned in the 23rd Psalm. The purpose of this book is to define, model, and explain this ancient methodology for true spiritual transformation. We can thank ancient cultures for leaving secrets embodied in stone and the fact we are living in a time where science is confirming ancient knowledge in the realm of genetics and quantum physics. This book is the result of a thirty-year quest for answers to the greatest inquiries on Earth.

Why are humans here on Earth? What is our true purpose? Finally, are we operating out of our full potential? During this journey, I went full circle. I started research of the Bible then left the Bible, and reviewed ancient cultures, books left out of the Bible, and many esoteric disciplines. During this time, I was a voracious researcher, and I had to synthesize ancient accounts cross cultures.

The most fascinating and debated story on Earth is the story of Jesus incarnating on Earth to demonstrate the power of the Spirit while in a human body. His complete life was a mystery, and the world are only privy to a miniscule amount of His early years and His last few years on the Earth. There are many vague areas in the Bible which do not describe exactly what He did in the desert for 40 days. Why was it so important for

Jesus too fast for 40 days in an extreme sunlit environment?

The purpose of this book is also to submit an analysis of events in the desert. In fact, I hope to decode ancient artifacts and glyphs to unlock the methodologies for activating our spiritual bodies. It is only possible through synthesizing ancient knowledge, which intersects into compatible themes leading to spiritual transformation. One thing we know is Jesus is not a liar, and He promised humans could do everything He demonstrated and more! Ancient spiritual transformation knowledge was once ubiquitous but was eradicated and hidden from the masses.

This ancient investigation has limitations by the fact no one is alive from ancient times to show us the true straight path. Although diverse ancient cultures spoke of the Most High, angels, and gods, we rely on stone tablets, bas-reliefs, and ancient narratives for insights into those who demonstrated Spirit power. We must meticulously review ancient artifacts and rely on intuitive revelation. Additionally, we can bridge knowledge from ancient orders, ancient sources, prophet accounts, and teachings of Christ juxtaposed with modern science for validations.

This book will use ancient artifacts to build a strong case the Sun used in conjunction with ancient methodologies result in the activation of our spiritual bodies. Opening humankind to a Spirit realm teeming with sentient beings and imbuing humans with amazing abilities. This book will also acknowledge Renaissance painters who embodied a secret in their work. I believe their art possess components to spiritual transformation, which hides in plain sight.

The Bible is clear the *Children of the Light* suffer from a lack of knowledge. We must ask ourselves what caused a lack of knowledge? Validations in this book require people to follow the teachings and methodologies from the ancient text, which includes the Bible. Then and only then will the ancient righteous path be irrefutable and hopefully will be practiced by all.

Our current religious systems cause spiritual atrophy and lead to zero cases of people demonstrating the Spirit's power. If this book presents any erroneous findings or concepts, it is my hope "the baby will not be thrown out with the bathwater," but correction and continued research will be the result. I would be remiss if I did not mention my late wife inspired me to begin writing and sharing knowledge with the world. When she was alive, I felt like the richest man on the Earth, and her Faith was steadfast and helped me focus on the teachings of Jesus.

Although this book meanders away from Jesus at times, it always finds its way back to Him. Reason being is the story of Christ, and the Disciples is the closest demonstration we have to the power of Spirit. His story is important not just because He is the Son of God, but because He comes from a part in space popularly known as Heaven located in Orion. Diverse ancient cultures either include (Harper, 2009) Orion in their Creation mythology or embodied Orion somehow in their artifacts.

Christ is royalty from the Orion Kingdom (Laura, 2011) and part of His mission on Earth was to show humanity the full potential of the human hybrid construct. We truly are spiritual beings having a human experience, and there are *keys* to unlocking spiritual abilities. Clear context and understanding is what this book's journey is all about! *If* just one of us can break through after reading this book that will lead others to spiritual transformation! I hope this book is the seed that grows into the spiritual oak tree for generations to climb.

I believe based on my research we are living at the end of an Age. The Mayans, December 21, 2012, was never about the end (Council, 2009) of the world. That was nothing but media spin. The Mayan's said we were at the end of the fourth world and entering the fifth world. Mayan prophecy believed this was the time humankind's signal would raise in the "tree of life" and achieving a higher consciousness would be possible.

For this to happen, we must turn away from those who promote what is not working. We are a world of followers that follow men and women with no power. These spiritual leaders rely on *wise* and *persuasive* words and practice emotional alchemy. It is time we reinvestigate ancient ways which yielded results in conformance with the teachings of Jesus.

The last human demonstration of man' spiritual potential. Many people today have confused emotional alchemy with the Holy Spirit. They believe being touched by the Holy Spirit is whipping their hair back and forth, then taking a nap on the altar. That is not the Holy Spirit, and there are no ancient accounts like this.

The Holy Spirit gives you great power, and you can demonstrate it by healing people, commanding angels, creating spontaneous matter, changing the form of matter, flying, teleporting, resurrection, and power over death, etc. These abilities sound like science fiction, but this is exactly what spiritually transformed humans were able to do. These spiritually transformed people appeared as gods to the uninitiated, but they were human. We all have the potential to do these very things based on what Jesus demonstrated to the world.

All we need is *one* person on the Earth to achieve spiritual transformation, and the rest will follow.

Ancient Proofs

Luke 17:21

21 Neither shall they say, Lo here! Or, lo there! For, behold, the kingdom of God is within you.

There are many clues in the ancient past describing something powerful and attainable hidden inside the human body. Once activated this hidden power has separated men from common men, and they became mysteries displaying abilities that can only define as godlike. When Christ said to people, "The kingdom is within" it was a mystery to the uninitiated. Christ knew the "secret," and there are many unanswered questions about His life from age twelve to thirty, including what He did while in the desert for forty days.

Artwork of Christ and His disciples in thirteenth and fourteenth century frequently illustrated disc shape halos directly behind their heads, which looks conspicuously like the Sun. These Divinity discs symbolized Spirit in the subject, but the artist also included the Sun and sometimes two Suns. Even the

St. John the Baptist, School: Byzantine;
Second half of the 13th-early 14th century
State Hermitage Museum, St, Petersburg

artist during those days knew the Sun's connection to these spiritually elevated men and women. Why was the Sun so important to Christ and His Disciples?

There is even a reference to the Sun in the Bible, in Ecclesiastes 11:7 it states, *"Light t is sweet, and it pleases the eyes to see the sun."* Additionally, the Ecclesiastes inverse 7:11 says, *"Wisdom, like an inheritance, is a good thing and benefits those who see the sun."*

The ancients were aware the Sun provided the human body a peaceful feeling, and we will circle back to this. The ancient also said something very profound and that is wisdom increases by gazing at the Sun! How is this possible? One thing we know for sure is the ancients were very aware of the power of the Sun and its effects on the human body.

John the Baptist was another major prophet who spent an exorbitant amount of time in the wilderness and the mountainous desert region. In fact, his ministry began in the desert, and he demonstrated the power of clairvoyance. These locations were perfect locations to Sungaze, and the artist illustrates him with the Sun behind his head or pointing up to it! Spiritual men who harnessed the power of the Sun through the optic nerve were set apart from society.

They were able to separate themselves from people who relied on the community for survival needs and thrive in inhospitable environments. Moses was led from a voice within and was shown the exact rock to strike to release fresh cold sweet spring water for the thirsty people. The ancient man was the last generation to demonstrate amazing abilities from within, and modern man has been unable to demonstrate one act they did on demand. Why is that?

The Sun disc was not only associated with males in the Bible it was also illustrated behind the heads of prominent women in the Bible. The mother of Christ, Mary, was depicted with the Sun disc behind her head. Mary Magdalene, was considered equal to the Disciples (she most likely was a Disciple) and her Gospel was not included in the Bible based on authenticity debates, I daresay because she was a woman! Davinci even painted her at *The Last Supper!* She too was illustrated with the Sun disc behind her head and thirteenth-century artwork illustrated this fact.

It should be clear the Sun played a major role in the spiritual transformation of major characters in the Bible and artists were certainly aware of this solar connection. It is apparent the Sun was a driving force in the spiritual development of these followers, and the Sun became a badge to identify them. We must also acknowledge the followers of Christ were despised and most of them were eventually hunted down and murdered. Common folk became threatened by those who transform spiritually.

The Crucifixion
Pacino di Bonaguida
1315-1320 century

In the artwork by Pacino di Bonaguida, you will notice the Holy women with the Sun disc behind their heads at the feet of the crucified Christ. It is also interesting to note two Sun symbols are on the left and the right of the cross. Again, we see the Sun disc behind the head of the Christ. It should be clear now that Sun has a connection to Spirit.

Mind you the background is black for night time, yet two Suns are displayed! I believe the ancients left us the secrets in plain view and the Vatican obscured these secrets for other reasons. There is another element that is critical before going before the Sun, and that is the condition of the human heart. All these Biblical examples of men and women with the Sun disc behind their heads followed Biblical moral practices and values.

These people were righteous, and their hearts were pure. All of them probably *lived* the Book of Proverbs. Emotion is said to be energy in motion and energy can be positively or negatively charged. The ancients believe you must have a positive heart to receive gifts from the Sun; while the negative hearts will stay trapped in the material world. Therefore, Jesus preached love and acceptance *without sin.*

I now trust being without sin is vital for the spiritual conversion process. Operating in sin means failure for those who hope to receive the Holy Spirit. This Sun and heart connection illustrate in voluminous Renaissance paintings of Christ. You will also encounter art from this time with the human heart inside the Sun.

Therefore, Christ emphasized love because without it the solar process would not cultivate the spirit and guarantee no results; while *any sin* would fill the human body with a negative charge. It also makes you wonder *if* the Sun is conscious. How does the Sun measure the heart of the observer?

Only a positive heart could process and mature through solar cultivation to become transformed. It should be no surprise Eastern spiritualist claims the *solar* plexus is the gateway to the heart. The heart gives a deeper insight into John 14:6, *"Jesus saith unto him, I am the way, the truth, and the life: no man cometh unto the Father, but by me."* Jesus taught a spiritual, behavioral matrix which conditioned the heart to be solar compliant.

It should be no surprise if the Sun could ignite the human heart with "fire" then it could also destroy it. Malachi 4:1-3, is aptly titled, "The Sun of Righteousness Will Dawn" and here it references a solar event, which will have horrific effects on the wicked; or those who never purified their hearts or sun gazed.

Malachi 4:1-3, goes on to say, *"Count on it: The day is coming, raging like a forest fire. All the arrogant people who do evil things will be burned up like stove wood, burned to a crisp, nothing left but scorched earth and ash— a black day. But for you, sunrise! The sun of righteousness will dawn on those who honor my name, healing radiating from its wings. You will be bursting with energy, like colts frisky and frolicking. And you'll tromp on the wicked. They'll be nothing but ashes under your feet on that Day." God-of-the-Angel-Armies says so."*

This ancient text speaks with bravado when it says, "Count on it!" If you think about it, Jesus did attempt to save the world by saving their hearts. It is the only way to survive the solar event, and it is only through His ways. Because Jesus comprehensively addressed the heart regulations through repentance, forgiveness, and love without sin. I believe Grace will protect those who never Sun gazed if their hearts are spiritually compliant.

Those who experience solar healing will be like "colts frisky and frolicking" on the Day of the Lord, according to Malachi 4:1-4. The Sun is the one thing people of the Earth cannot avoid nor escape. No matter how deep humankind burrows into the Earth, the tectonic plates will always be affected by solar flares.

There is even a correlation between solar flares weather and earthquakes.

The Sun is another thing every eye on Earth can see. The Sun has a major role in prophecy when reading the Bible, but have you noticed it is the least discussed prophetic event by the modern-day church? Prosperity preachers have profited off snippets of ancient teachings, but none of them drive you to spiritually transforming yourself with the Sun. Every major Biblical character followed an ancient path, which included the Sun.

On the next page is a stained-glass painting of Christ with the Sun behind His head and He is pointing to His heart. You will see His heart wrapped in "thorns" and "flames" licking out the top of His heart. There is also the symbol of the Sun around the heart. The Sun commonly painted with "thorns" illustrating the solar rays relationship to the heart.

The flames are related to the solar rays (Marshall, 2014) and they will ignite the heart of the person. Can you imagine your heart changing and becoming on fire with peace, love, and spiritual knowledge? Perhaps, even communicating with Heavenly beings? What about

the solar cross behind His head on the stained-glass painting of Jesus?

The dogwood cross is where there is a divergence away from the original meaning of the solar cross. December 2009, I discovered a correlation between a frequency in a cymatic experiment and the Tablet of Shamash. This experiment consisted of beach sand on a steel plate fastened to a tone generator. When the tone generator produced a tone, the sand would form into a geometric shape.

The symbol on the tablet of Shamash was remarkably similar to a cymatic I witnessed in an array of tones in a video. My oversight was not seeing just the Sun as a symbol. Furthermore, the Sun surely has its own frequency based on tone measurement. I produced a video short titled, *Secret of the Sumerian Tablet* on YouTube, but in retrospect, the cymatic was not a hundred-percent perfect match for the symbol of the Sun.

The solar cross symbols are also showing us the ultraviolet radiation emanating from the Sun. It also shows us a compass with a north, south, east, and west. The symbol illustrates energy radiating from the Sun travels in all directions. This solar cross is part of a mystery involving frequency, but there is also a relationship to spiritual life and death on the cross.

People teach the cruxifcation of Christ was on the Roman cross. While the Romans were infamous for crucifying criminals on a cross, there was another cross prior to this Roman cross with a Divine purpose.

Sun on shield | Tone cymatic

Tablet of Shamash - 9th century B.C.

Meaning the cross has an ancient origin in respect to its transformative capabilities for the human body in conjunction with the Sun. We will circle back to this in detail later in this book!

If we trace back to the earliest iterations of the cross, we must visit the ancient Sumerian culture located in Mesopotamia, and we will see an element of the ankh cross design. The cross design would be the ring which is held by the seated giant seen in, "The Tablet of Shamash," his name translates to "the Sun" hence the name "the Sun god." As the Sun-god there were many hymns attributed to him. One of the hymns that stand out praises the sun god's all-seeing nature as "Illuminator of All."

I believe this is the connection to the Sun activating the pineal gland which sets off a chain reaction in the endocrine system of the human body. This phrase, "illuminator of all" is not just talking about light. It has another meaning, and I believe it means, "spiritual or intellectual enlightenment." Is it possible the Sun is conditioning and transitioning mechanism to human wisdom? The Bible certainly says so!

Although the Sun is the sustainer of life in modern times, its anciently known capabilities are not understood. One of the most popular Biblical character's imbues with superhuman strength and links to the Sun. The name Samson is a Hebrew name. In Hebrew, the meaning of the name Samson is: "Sun child; bright sun." Samson translates from the Hebrew word Shamash which means Sun. Samson translates to "little Sun." The

Sumerian and Babylonian Sun god was called Shamash.

If Shamash from the Babylonian era was a truly pagan name, why would the Most High imbue Samson (little Sun) with enough power to rip a lion apart like a rotisserie chicken? I believe it's possible ancient man did not worship the Sun but used the Sun as a tool for spiritual transformation. If the Sun is "pagan" why would the Most High endorse a man named after the Sun?

If we recap, we begin to see some of the components for solar activation for humankind: Sun, the ring, the staff, and the pineal gland. We also see a relationship between the Sumerian/Babylonian Sun god and Samson in the Bible for *strength* and *wisdom*. There are utility and application for "thy rod" and "thy staff." In the tablet of Shamash, you will see solar rays coursing through the body of the seated giant.

Shamash was able to "eat" the Sun. The concept of "eating" the Sun, cannot be the actual Sun he was eating, but (rays) like a plant synthesizing energy like a photovoltaic effect on the human body. There is also a cymatic element to this tablet with the Sun symbol on a shield. Additionally, those glyphs in the floor below and above represent frozen frequencies.

These contextual concepts certainly correlate with the formula of *sound* and *light* for creation in the Bible! Remember, in the beginning, was *sound* and then *light*, hence the creation process was initiated using frequency and light. The Sun god, Shamash, was able to travel great distances without relying on food sources because he would draw energy from the Sun. Later in the book, you will see Jesus did the same thing.

Shamash is one of the earliest, if not the earliest account of a god who fed off the Sun for sustenance. Analyzing the Tablet of Shamash, you also see the Sun on a table, and the symbol displays elements which support modern scientific understanding of the Sun. There is a compass showing the cardinal directions of the Sun. Like Earth, the Sun has the North Pole, the South Pole, and an equator.

The poles of the Sun are different in several ways from the areas near the Sun's equator. The Sun has a magnetic field with North and South magnetic poles. About every 11 years, the (Wall, 2013) Sun's magnetic poles flip – North becomes South and vice versa." The Sumerian civilization is shrouded in mystery because it sprang forth in Mesopotamia, with the first writing, mathematics, science, politics, and art, etc. Was this a

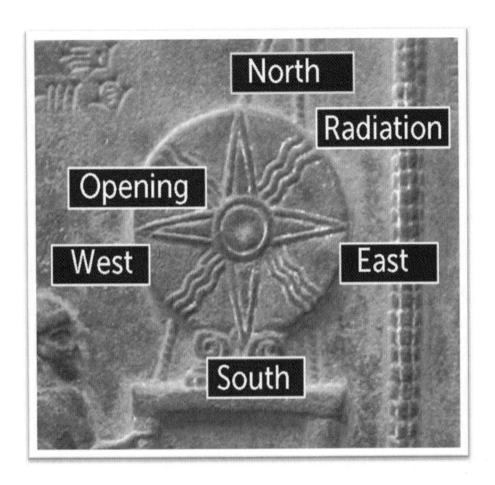

culture of Sun gazers who tapped into Universal knowledge as a result?

It is very telling the Sumerian culture had a hero that relied on the Sun to prosper! The people of Sumerian where called, "Sag-Giga" translated as, "The Black-headed people" and I believe were dark-skinned people. The Assyrians used Ashur, to represent the Sun and much like logos today, he demonstrated through art the capabilities of the Sun. Many people have missed the true meaning of Ashur and until recently, even myself.

It is easy to be erroneously influenced by peers and established academia, however, once you adopt the ancient solar perspective you gain ancient insights. The Sun interacts with humans and integrates solar elements *within* the human body. There are also many parallels between the Sumerians who began in 4,000 BC and Christian accounts, where Job is the oldest book in the Bible written in 1,500 BC. The Sumerians have, "Seven Tablets of Creation" including an Abraham and a Sarai. Their "Epic of Gilgamesh" references a destructive world flood, thousands of years before the Biblical accounts.

There is also a reference to Shamash Sungazing, (RELIGIOUS SUNGAZING, n.d.) Tablet X, says, *"No man has ever gone that way and lived to say he crossed the sea. Shamash only ventures there, only Shamash would dare to stare into the sun."* The Sun god Shamash passed the Code of Hammurabi directly to the King of Babylon, to govern the people dating back to 1754 BC. Both the Sumerians, Egyptians, and the Christians share a "cross" like object, which associates with godhood. The difference with Christianity is Jesus Christ was considered the Son of God, is part of the Godhead, and King of Kings.

Of course, Jesus has many similarities with Horus of ancient Egypt! The only time Christ was known to carry a cross was on His long march to His death, but He is painted carrying a staff. This rod and staff have a role in the transformative process of solar spiritual transformation. Please note how none of the Disciples were overly concerned with their deaths after witnessing the resurrection.

Did witnessing firsthand the teachings of Christ powered by the Sun teach them they could transcend death? Many people will claim I am suggesting Sun worship, but that is not an accurate assessment. Sungazing is no more Sun worship than a person going to the beach and *using* the Sun to get a tan. If for some reason our modern world was destroyed and thousands of years later archeologist rediscovered chains of tanning salons.

Would it be accurate to claim that tanning salons were Sun worship temples? The ancients knew the Sun had a purpose within man and it could act as a catalyst for making a man reach full potential spiritually. Spirit power is part of what Jesus came to demonstrate to us, and the Sun was part of His evolution to demonstrating great power from *within*, while in a human body. We must reexamine academic meta-data and conclusions regarding ancient artifacts and practices in ancient times.

I encountered many arguments that claim Jesus was not real or He was only a representation of the Sun. The conclusion Jesus was not real, is an erroneous thought process because if we accept the examples and teachings of Jesus at face value, there is a spiritual methodology for transformation. Jesus demonstrated the perfect emotion of love energy without sin and a framework for human activation to Spirit. Even the account of Jesus laying down His life for the sins of the world was an act of love.

Furthermore, how do you even begin to explain away the prophecy in the Bible? These are tangible events with causation clearly outlined in Biblical prophecy. One of my favorites is Revelation 16:12, "*And the sixth angel poured out his vial upon the great river the Euphrates; and the water thereof was dried up, that the way of the kings of the east might be prepared.*" It is traditionally accepted the book of Revelation was written near the end of the first century, around A.D. 96.

On July 13, 2009, the New York Times (Robertson, Campbell, 2009) published the story of the Euphrates River is drying up! My point here is people can compare Jesus to Horus, Krishna, Mithra, and Dionysius, but Biblical prophecy can never be jettisoned. The real curiosity should be how these humans *demonstrated* godlike abilities.

There appears to be short-sighted and a limiting perspective regarding the Sun. There is an ancient footprint, which represents a systematic approach to incorporating Sun gazing for the benefit of our collective spiritual cultivation. The first step is accepting Jesus Christ as a subject matter expert on the spiritual transformation! If we can accept there is a Spiritual Kingdom, does it not make sense emissaries were sent over time to teach humans about their spiritual selves?

What makes Jesus different from all the others is His death created a wormhole back to the Heavenly Kingdom upon death for human souls. The Egyptian Book of the Dead stated spirit travel was possible to another realm. Without following the methodology of the ancients, humans will never realize the Spirit power demonstrated by men of yore. Before the creation of the Bible, various ancient cultures recognized the Sun was key for spiritual upgrades for personal developments, wisdom, laws, peace, and communication with the Heavenly realm.

According to these ancient cultures, the Sun was the gateway to the Creator, and the only way was through the Sun. Where have we heard this before? John 14:6, *"Jesus saith unto him, I am the way, the truth, and the life: no man cometh unto the Father, but by me."* The Bible is coded, and there is a dichotomy in his statement where you must follow the Son's ways, and you must use the Sun to cultivate yourself spiritually.

There is more from John 12:36, where he says, *"Those who receive the light become children of light."* I believe we can insert the word "Sun" in front of the light to make *sunlight*. Now, these ancient statements are making more sense once we juxtapose them against the Renaissance art of solar disc behind the head of Christ and His Disciples. In John 1:8, he stated something very profound, *"He was not that Light, but was sent to bear witness of that Light."*

We know the Most High is more than just "Light".

Christ came to demonstrate the heart and Sun connection to Spirit so that we could break the chains of hidden knowledge controlled by the Pharisees. The Rigveda, the oldest of the Vedas sacred texts composed between 1,500 and 1,000 BCE, introduces the Hindu Sun god, Surya. There are interesting similarities between the Sumerian illustrations of the Sun and the Rigveda.

Surya illustrated as a red man with three eyes and four arms; he rides a chariot drawn by seven mares. Finally, Surya is holding water lilies in each hand. Do we see another symbol of something that comes out of the Sun that is beneficial to humanity? The four arms are the cardinality directions of the Sun having a North and a South Magnetic Pole.

We can also deduce the three eyes representing one for the Sun, one for the observer, and one for the pineal gland of the human being. The seven mares represent Surya's solar delivery system, which activates the seven energy points of the human body. All these cultures have a different name for the Sun, but when you break down their attributes you certainly, find common themes! Further analysis shows Surya with a *ring* hovering above his finger pointing up.

Remember the Sumerian hero Shamash known as the "Sun god" was also holding a ring. Surya looks to be holding a bottle, but usually, this is illustrated as a conch shell and speaks to sound. Again, we are reintroduced to sound and light as part of a birthing process to something new. Do you see how the Bible is coded?

Do you understand how ideas can be twisted to no

longer see the pink elephant in the room? If we fast forward to ancient Egypt, we will see the next iteration of the cross, and it is called the ankh. This ancient Egyptian ankh is a ubiquitous symbol on many relief walls in the hands of gods and goddesses. The ankh defines in the hieroglyphic dictionary as a symbol as the "key of life" and also as "power symbols" for royalty.

Why would the gods/goddesses carry an object on their person with no utility? The ankh was also one of the earliest symbols for Christianity, and that should be no surprise since Christianity birthed on the banks of the Nile. Most of the ancient Egyptian pantheon illustrate holding a was-scepter in one hand, and an ankh in the other with the Sun depicted above their head. Does this sound familiar?

I believe what we are seeing is an application when it comes to the ankh and the was-scepter. The ancient Egyptians usually illustrated the Sun in some form with the ankh and the was-scepter. The further the time distanced away from ancient Egypt the more the ankh became modified to the Christian cross we have today. I believe the ankh was powered by low voltage electricity and in the hand of a highly melanated person, an oscillating field morphed around the human body.

Early Christian stela incorporating a looped cross (crux ansata) or ankh symbol, surrounded by the vine of eternal life, illustrating the fusion of pharaonic iconography with Christian motifs in Byzantine Egypt. Country of Origin: Egypt Culture Coptic Date/Period: 4th-7th Century AD Metropolitan Museum of New York

This might sound farfetched but: Albertus B. Mostert, Benjamin J. Powell, Francis L. Pratt, Graeme R. Hanson, Tadeusz Sarna, Ian R. Gentle, and Paul

Meredith (Albertus B. Mostert, 2012) completed a study of this very thing titled, "Role of semiconductivity and ion transport in the electrical conduction of melanin."

The abstract stated, *"Melanins are pigmentary macromolecules found throughout the biosphere that, in the 1970s, was discovered to conduct electricity and display bistable switching. Since then, it has been widely believed that melanins are naturally occurring amorphous organic semiconductors."* One the most unheralded inventors in the world is Nicholas Tesla. Even Tesla built electric devices from the design specifications of the ankh. The ankh is an oscillator, which allowed low voltage current to flow through the melanated skin of the human body.

The batteries in ancient Egypt operated below 1 volt, but that was sustainable and most likely did not damage the DNA. I compare these ancient batteries to the (Meyerhoff, 2000) Bagdad battery. We will explore the effects on our DNA later in the book. We can see before Christianity the cross was distinctly unique from the current iteration.

We can safely say this current cross is not an oscillator. The meaning of the modern cross is

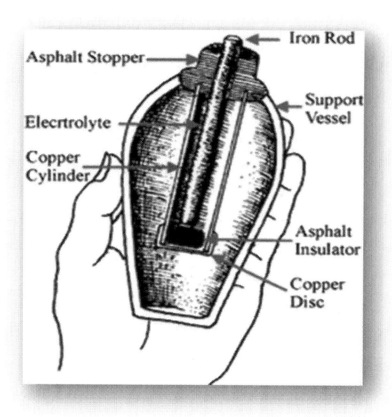

symbolic of the crucifixion and Christianity. The average person is none the wiser that the original cross, was utilitarian and the ancients continually illustrated this fact in the hands of their gods or goddesses because it had an application. The earliest illustrations the cross was just a ring with a bar in the hand of the Sumerian hero Shamash.

It progressively matured into an ankh and the powerless cross of today. The Egyptian ankh combines with a djed, which is classically defined as a

Ankh   Battery   Was-Scepter

the pillar-like symbol in hieroglyphics representing stability. However, as research on the djed symbol progressively matured some believe it was a battery (like Tesla coils) used to power devices, including the ankh. Murals by Nsut Bety (Pharaoh) Seti I in Abydu (Abydos) in 1290 BCE illustrate the battery djed.

The was-scepter is also illustrated with the djed. Why would an ankh need a battery? There was a rumor Napoleon (1798-1801) was on a scientific expedition to Egypt where he recovered an operational ankh and it was powered by a battery. What are the chances a year after Napoleon's scientific expedition the first

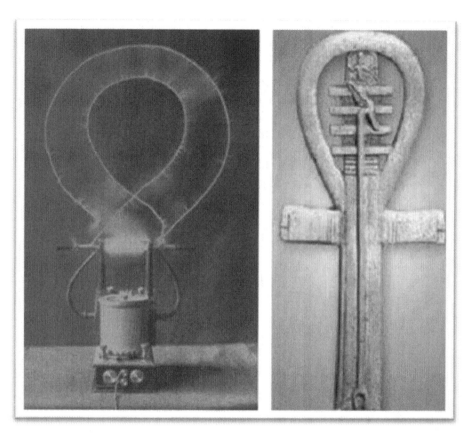

The djed is assembled inside the loop of the ankh with was-scepter included. Suggesting that these are used together.

patent for the circuit was filed? The ancients were more advanced then people give them credit for and I believe the low voltage ankh is evidence of one of many. I am purposely not delving into Sun worship because I believe academics have misinterpreted the ancient past regarding Sun worship. I am sure some people did go off the deep end and worship the Sun, just as some modern-day folk believes the Earth to be flat.

To that end, it means there had to be Sungazers who saw the Sun as a tool to facilitate change inside the human body and awaken Spiritual capabilities. Zechariah Sitchin was once the go-to translator for Sumerian cuneiform, but he humanized interpretations that should be questioned. Suppose thousands of years from now Disney World is excavated and soon the academic narrative turns into there was a highly worshiped humanoid mouse god who had a wonderful sense of style! This is exactly what Sitchin did with Sumerian personalities and also fueled the ancient astronaut belief.

A few researchers asserted the Sun god Ashur was an old space explorer in a flying machine. What the ancients did was use the Sun to activate the "Kingdom" within and spiritually cultivate themselves to receive the Holy Spirit. The ancients also communicated with the Heavenly realm. Communicating with Spirit beings explains the "advanced" knowledge used to create edifices modern technology still cannot achieve.

It seems modern man externalized his search for advanced life when the ancients had demonstrated the

Assyrian symbol of the Sun using Ashur

 The Sun with rays radiating outward. Ashur is beckoning to look into his eyes. He holds a ring in his left hand.

 The Sun is no longer radiating rays outward. Now it is open and aims to shoot the "dove" out.

connection to advanced life is achieved from within us. I did not cover every ancient civilization that had some form of Sun deity or labeling of Sun worship. There are too many to discuss in one chapter, but I hope I successfully presented enough of the ancient past to show you Sungazing was key to human spiritual development before even Christ incarnated on the Earth.

Our great ancient Teacher had to re-demonstrate the formula of how to activate spiritual transformation in the human body. As you progress through this book, it is my hope you revisit everything you have learned regarding religion using *solar glasses*. I have no doubt some ancient cultures worshiped the Sun. These were obvious misled people who exchanged a lie for the truth.

Much like the remnant of modern people who believe the Earth is flat. The ancients understood the Law of Duality, which means everything has a dual purpose. Which means our Sun is more than meets the eye. The Sun is the male energy that impregnates the mother Earth, and we witnessed the physical manifestations of an invisible process.

The same holds true for a man where the Sun harvests the invisible Spirit inside man. We have examples of DNA resequence in caterpillars as they transform into butterfly species. Would the Most High make butterflies greater than man? The ancients that graduated the spiritual process were humans just like us and archeologist have yet to find non-human "god" DNA.

Once these ancient humans became spiritually activated they were no longer considered human, but gods. Just like a butterfly who was no longer considered a caterpillar. I admit the Most High did not make the process easy, where we go to sleep, form a pupa and emerge from chrysalis a butterfly. I do believe our spirit is sleeping now.

Jesus demonstrated to follow His strict ways, and this is a major hurdle for many people, but the door is always open, as long as the Sun is shining.

Religious Art and the Son/Sun

"Use a picture. It's worth a thousand words."
- Tess Flanders (circa 1911)

Art is the evidence of imagination, events, ideology, beliefs, and frames human perspectives for posterity. Art is subjective to the observer but rises above the commentary and consensus of popular culture, including religious dogma. The Earth is blessed to have so many talented artists from various cultures, but one period captures the solar relationship to spiritual cultivation and a mysteries location in space. Renaissance artwork embodied in paintings, frescos, mandylions, and stelas, which captured the hidden elements to human spiritual completion.

Most if not all the prominent Bible characters are illustrated with the Sun disc behind their heads. The Sun disc transcended gender because it was the spiritual symbol to reflect that person operated in the highest state of Spirit. They were different from other humans who did not have access to Spirit! How is it possible artist from different countries painted the solar symbol behind the heads of Biblical characters?

Why did the artist choose to capture the solar disc emanating from the head? I do not believe the halo only represented Divinity, but it also represented the Sun. There is a biological connection we will delve into later in this book. The purpose of this chapter is to introduce the art of this time, and prove the Sun is the key transformation element for our spiritual cultivation.

It will also prove this is not Sun worship, because Jesus, being part of the Godhead endorsed gazing at the Sun in the Bible. Furthermore, wearing solar colored glasses will allow you to see the references to the Sun and Christ also came to testify about the Light. Later in the book, we will discuss why these keys of knowledge were removed, reinterpreted for the masses, and hidden in plain view.

You will see more than just the Sun in this artwork, but a concerted effort to illustrate pointing at the Sun, looking at the Sun, and receiving flowers, cake, ale, and doves from the Sun. All these things are coming out of the Sun actually "shoot" into people according to the Ashur the Sun god tablet! Therefore, the ancient artist illustrated a bow and arrow to deliver the solar gift. You will see this very thing in the Assyrian tablet of Ashur using the bow to send a "flower" or dove shape out of the Sun.

I will note there was not an arrowhead illustrated on the end of the arrow because this is not a destructive action. You will see religious art where the artist features the classical halo, but also the Sun prominently placed in the painting. Lending credence to the plausibility the Sun was more than just a symbol for Divinity but a key tool for spiritual transformation. Here is the classical definition of the halo in art:

A halo (from Greek ἅλως, halōs; [1] also known as a nimbus, aureole, glory, or gloriole) is a crown of light rays, circle or disc of light that surrounds a person in the art. They have been used in the iconography of many religions to indicate holy or sacred figures and have at various periods also been used in images of rulers or heroes.

In the sacred art of Ancient Greece, Ancient Rome, Hinduism, Buddhism, Islam, and Christianity, among other religions, sacred persons may be depicted with a halo in the form of circular glow, or flames in Asian art, around the head or around the whole body—this last one often called a mandorla. Halos may be shown as almost any color or combination of colors, but are most often depicted as golden, yellow or white when representing light or red when representing flames. (Halo (religious iconography), 2007)

Icon of the Holy Mandylion of Christ
1st half of 13th century

Please note we see the Sun and cardinal points like we saw on the "Tablet of Shamash." We also see the solar rays streaking down and of course, we see a rendition of Jesus Christ. This is not a halo as many people have been led to believe by popular culture, but the Sun. I think it is also interesting there are arrows pointing down as well!

"Adoration of the Magi"
Giotto di Bondone,
Florence, Italy
1266 – 1337

Again, we see solar disc behind the heads of key Biblical characters including the angel standing by baby Jesus.

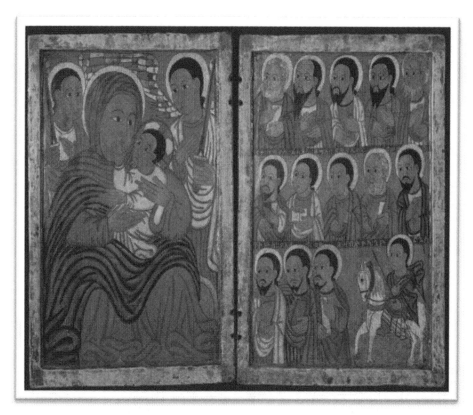

**Diptych with Mary and Her Son Flanked by
Archangels, Apostles, and a Saint**
Ethiopia
15th century, tempera on wood

The pattern continues of the artist illustrating all characters with the Sun behind their heads. It is safe to assume the Sun is key to all spiritual cultivation including the angel in the picture. Every Disciple appears to have Sun gazed long enough to have their pineal gland activated. It should be clear the Sun is vital for spiritual advancement.

Habakkuk the Spiritual Warrior
Contemporary Medieval painting

What is fascinating about this painting is the artist made the spiritual warrior Habakkuk point directly at the Sun behind his head. This illustrates the importance of the Sun in becoming a spiritual warrior. Can you deny these artists did not know the importance of the Sun and that it was a key element to spiritual power? This looks too much like the Sun. Do you agree?

ASSUNZIONE - Rise of the Mother of God Christ
Pantokrator's Church in High Dechanakh (Serbia, Kosovo)
1335-1350

This painting places Mother Mary in the Sun with the Sun behind her head. Even the angels have the Sun behind their heads showing us the importance of the Sun. Is this art suggesting a means of communication with spiritual beings through the Sun?

Unknown

This painting is fascinating, and unfortunately, I could not track down the details, but I could not leave it out. Again, we see the Sun playing its role in the spiritual background, and we also see other beings behind the Sun. This is very telling because it is saying "through the Sun" we can communicate with Heavenly beings. The artist even painted the Sun behind the head of Mary Magdalene to illustrate she was solar activated. Please note the Sun cannot be confused with a halo in this piece.

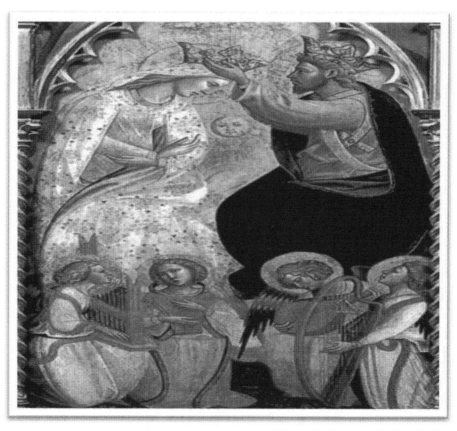

Incoronazione della Vergine e Santi (Firenze)
Giovanni Giovanni dal Ponte
Galleria dell'Accademia, Firenzedal Ponte
1400-1410

This painting is teaching us it is not just the Sun that is the catalyst, but *sound* for our spiritual transformation. Again, we see the Sun prominently placed in the painting and humbleness to Mary who is being crowned. This is another case of the Sun being featured; while not being confused with a halo by the artist.

Prophet Elijah from a two-sided icon
Late 12th century
Image courtesy of the Byzantine Museum, Kastoria

Elijah began his ministry 870 years before Christ, and we see the Sun is associated with his spiritual development. Elijah was a major prophet, and it is even prophesied he will return in the last days. Do you agree this artist realized the importance of the Sun and its key transformation role in the spiritual cultivation of mankind?

St. Apostle Peter
Visoki Dečani
Kosovo, Serbia
14th Century

Peter was another one of the Disciples of Christ who Jesus predicted to deny Him three times, but he went on to do amazing things in the Bible. This painter chose colors to perfectly match the Sun.

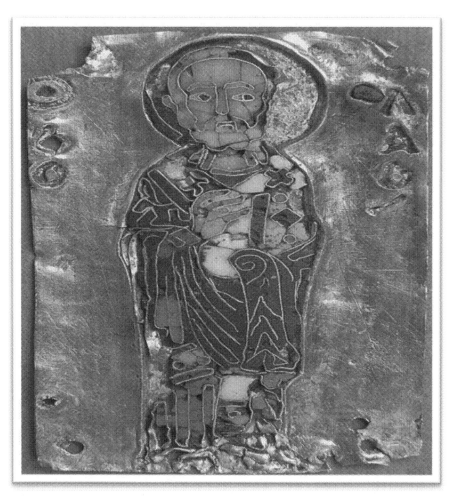

Medallion of St. Nicholas (Byzantine)
Courtesy of The Met
11th century

St. Nicholas was a Christian bishop who helped the needy. Born in Patara, a land that is part of present-day Turkey, circa 280. Again, we see the Sun behind the head of the spiritually advanced follower of the teachings of Christ.

The Assembly of the Archangels
Byzantine, Constantinople or Crete
Tempera on gold ground and gesso on wood
Late 15th century

This reminds me of the movie, "City of Angels" with Nicholas Cage and Meg Ryan. Where Nicholas Cage, played an angel and at sunset, all of the angels would gather at the beach to Sun gaze. All of the angels in this painting have the Sun behind their head as they escort Jesus Christ who also has the Sun behind His head. It appears as if the angels are presenting Christ as the Son/Sun King!

Crucifixion
Peter Gertner
The Walters Museum
1537

Looking into the crowd you will see the artist neglect to paint the Sun behind the heads of people in the crowd. Even the Pharisees have no Sun behind their head further emphasizing they were not part of the Kingdom of Christ. All the Disciples and the mother of Christ and Mary Magdalene with the Sun painted behind their heads.

The Pentecost
Girolamo da Carpi
1530 c.

Girolamo da Carpi, has illustrated an event involving the Sun where like the Sumerian Ashur showed the Sun with a hole in it and the dove shooting out. In this case, it is a dove and solar rays. Do you see the connection to the Assyrian Sun god tablet?

Arithmologia or from the shrine of the numbers
Athanasius Kircher
c. 1665

Athanasius Kircher, S.J., was a German Jesuit scholar and polymath who published around 40 major works, most notably in the fields of comparative religion, geology, and medicine. Here he shows the connection between our Sun and Sirius, Betelgeuse, and Procyon, the primary stars in the three constellations of Canis Major, Orion, and Canis Minor.

Musurgia Universalis
Athanasius Kircher
c. 1650

Athanasius Kircher, illustrating that through the Sun is access to the Heavenly realms in Orion. The Winter Triangle constellation symbol is used to identify Orion. Through Sun gazing communication can be established with the Heavenly realms and constructive knowledge can be gained.

Pentecostés
Pier Francesco Mazzucchelli
Castello Sforzesco, Milan
c. 1650

Pier Francesco Mazzucchelli (commonly known as il Morazzone; 1573–1626) was an Italian painter and draughtsman who was active in Milan. Again, we see the doves shooting out of the Sun and because it is Pentecost we know they entered the bodies of the Disciples.

Last Supper Tempera
Duccio Di Buoninsegna
1257-1318, Italy

Duccio di Buoninsegna, was an Italian painter active in
Siena, Tuscany, in the late 13th and early 14th
centuries. He was hired throughout his life to complete
many important works in government and religious
buildings around Italy. I am assuming the other
Disciples do not have Sun disc because it would have
obscured the art on the table.

The Temptation of St. Anthony
Tintoretto
1577

Tintoretto, was an Italian painter and a notable exponent of the Renaissance school. Again, we see the Sun playing a key role in the temptation of St. Anthony. We also see an angel exit the Sun and again we see the ring. I trust this artist knew the Sun was also a portal from which Heavenly beings could provide support and interact with humanity. We can also assume because St. Anthony was in prayer position he was communicating with the Heavenly realm and help was sent.

Battesimo Giovanni di Cristo
Gaulle detto il Bacicci
c. 1690

Battista Gaulli called il Baciccio or il Baciccia
(Genoa, 8 May 1639 - Rome, 2 April 1709) was an Italian
painter. Notice how Giovan paints a perfect circle to
represent the Sun? He then illustrates Heavenly beings
emanating from the Sun showing us the Sun was
operating over Christ and then within Christ!

St. John the Baptist
Leonardo da Vinci
c. 1513-1516

Leonardo da Vinci was an Italian Renaissance polymath whose areas of interest included invention, painting, sculpting, architecture, science, music, mathematics, engineering, literature, anatomy, geology, astronomy, botany, writing, history, and cartography. Interesting that John the Baptist is pointing up because he knew how to use the Sun to cultivate himself spiritually and he was in communication with the Heavenly realm through the Sun.

Out of all the artwork, this painting resonates with me the most. The smirk on the face of John the Baptist is very knowing. As if he has a secret and is not sharing it. Some will say he is pointing to Heaven and though that is plausible, it is 8.611 light years away. The Sun is directly overhead, and it is the closest celestial object which gives life to the Earth.

You have witnessed several Renaissance painters who featured classically accepted Divine halos behind the heads of prominent Biblical personalities. There is a connection between the Sun and the pineal gland in earning these halos. Many of the painters mentioned here went a step further and positioned the Sun as a component of spiritual manifestation. I trust these artists knew the secret of spiritual transformation and knew sharing the secret could lead to death.

The Vatican was the financier of this movement but also feared at the same time because they were merchants of mass death.

Hiding the Keys

Gospel of Thomas 5

Jesus said, *"Recognize what is in your sight, and that which is hidden from you will become plain to you. For there is nothing hidden which will not become manifest."*

The Bible makes a poignant statement in, 2 Corinthians 4:4 (KJV), where it says, *"In whom the god of this world hath blinded the minds of them which believe not, lest the light of the glorious gospel of Christ, who is the image of God, should shine unto them."* It explains the *minds* of the people of our world are *blind*. Now that you have a better understanding of the key role the Sun plays in our spiritual cultivation (from the earlier chapter) you understand this verse. What number of individuals do you know who accept utilizing the Sun to transform themselves spiritually?

Most of the world is blind to the fact the Sun transforms our minds and allows us to communicate with another world, a spiritual world thousands of light years away. Next, we experience a coded piece of the Scripture where it references the "light" of the glorious gospel of Christ who is the image of God. Finally, we get a direct reference to the Sun "shining" unto them. How did this former resident of the Heavenly realm "blind the minds?"

It makes perfect sense the adversaries to spiritual transformation would disconnect true spiritual development for the world. This plan insured humankind would never realize spiritual transformation. How else could the god of this world guarantee control of spiritual development? The "fallen" angels hid the knowledge of the Sun's relationship to not just our spiritual cultivation, but to the fact, we could communicate with Heavenly beings, if we are to believe the coded messages from Renaissance Holy paintings.

We should revisit ancient accounts of solar deities because there are tangible secrets encoded in them. Even the Bible has prominent characters named after the Sun, and many demonstrated superhuman strength. The Hebrew name for Sampson derives from the Hebrew word šemeš, which means "sun" so that Samson bore the name of God, who is called "a sun and shield." Perhaps, this gives new insight into Psalm 84:11, "For the LORD God is a *sun and shield*: the LORD will give grace and glory: no good thing will he withhold from them that walk uprightly."

The Sun has a guilty history as being solely worshiped as a light in the sky by some ancient cultures. I believe prophets who spent time in the wilderness knew to incorporate Sun gazing into spiritual transformation. Is it possible overtime this knowledge was lost, and the Spiritual Kingdom would send Teachers to re-educate humankind? John the Baptist and Jesus brought the focus back to the Light.

Indeed, Jesus testified to the "Light" in the Bible. Lucky for us some ancient artifacts left intact allow us to "see" the solar formula. Nowadays the Sun has been vilified and labeled cancer to human existence. Modern man fears the Sun and covers its eyes with tinted lenses. Yet, the ancients celebrated the Sun and embodied the Sun's powers in stone for later generations.

Who is the culprit for oppressing the Sun's role in our modern spiritual cultivation? All roads lead to the Vatican who was the ruling body over all churches, before the church split. I suspect a Vatican reformation to codify and omit the keys to not just spiritual development, but the solar communication pathways to the Heavenly realms in Orion and Pleiades. For example,

Athanasius Kircher, (2 May 1602 – 28 November 1680), was a highly esteemed Jesuit trained scholar.

Kircher (Rowland, 2002) too prominently codified the truth of our Sun's connection with Orion. Kircher published around 40 major works, most notably in the fields of comparative religion, geology, and medicine. Kircher, compared to fellow Jesuit Roger Boscovich and to Leonardo da Vinci for his voluminous range of interests, and honored with the title "Master of a Hundred Arts." It is safe to assume Kircher was merely following the mandates of the Papacy.

What is clear is through the art of Kircher is he *codified* the keys to knowledge. If Christ was on the Earth during this time He would have had the same issues with the Vatican; he had with the Pharisees. In Luke 11:52, Christ, addressed the Pharisees and said, *"Woe unto you, lawyers! for ye have taken away the key of knowledge: ye entered not in yourselves and them that were entering in ye hindered."* What are these hidden *keys* of knowledge?

If the Vatican is not serving the spiritual interest of the people, then whom is it serving? Why would the Holy See unplug the knowledge of the Sun's role for spiritual cultivation? We must assume when the pineal gland activates we no longer would rely on the Earthly administration. The hiding of the keys of knowledge preserved the riches of the Vatican and its future.

The Vatican separated the Heavenly realm and the Earthly realm and claimed to be the intercessor to the Most High. We know from Luke 11:52 this made Christ extremely angry and it was wrong then and it is wrong now. It should be clear that Church pressure to obscure religious imagery affected art from the 1530s (and on) resulted in the decrees of the final session of the Council of Trent in 1563. Including short and rather inexplicit passages concerning religious images, which were to have a great impact on the development of Catholic art. (Catholic Church art, 2018)

There were art driven religious guidelines mandated to control the perceptions of the masses based on Papal initiatives (Jaroslav Jan Pelikan, n.d.). Much traditional iconography considered without adequate scriptural foundation was prohibited, *as was any inclusion of classical pagan elements in religious art,* and almost all nudity, including that of the infant Jesus. From this, we understand how Vatican initiatives shaped the tapestry of art (as we know it today) and as the teachings in the church promoted Christ they omitted a special key to His spiritual cultivation in human form, which is the Sun. It should be obvious to you the Vatican codified what Christ came to teach which encodes in various art forms financed by the Vatican.

Humans have access to the Heavenly realms through solar spiritual cultivation and activation of the pineal gland. In 1209 to 1229, there was a community in Southern France that included Sun gazing for spiritual cultivation, based on the practices of Jesus and His Disciples. They were the Cathars and were not worshiping the Sun but using it as Christ and Prophets of the Bible demonstrated. Pope Innocent III decreed the Cathars, a heretical sect and staked gold and other pleasures for three thousand crusaders to savagely murder them and anyone who supported them. (Purdin, 2014)

From 1209-1249 one of the worst genocides in history was conducted against the Cathars, a heretical sect in southern France. Pope Innocent III, promising gold and indulgences (the remission of punishment due for sins) in exchange for the blood of the Cathars, sent 30,000 crusaders into France to massacre the Cathars and their supporters. The Cathars were hunted, tortured, burned at the stake and savagely murdered by the Church's hired killers. Estimates place the total number of Cathars and sympathizers murdered between 300,000 and 1,000,000 men, women and children. Throughout this bloodbath, an amazing phenomenon was witnessed. The Cathars did not express fear, anger or pain, but only bliss, despite the most horrendous atrocities committed against them. What did they know? - Wayne Purdin

The Cathars were stabbed, decapitated, tortured, and burned at the stake, yet they happily left the physical realm. The estimated number of people murdered was between three hundred thousand and one million: *men, women, and children.* Raphael Lemkin, who in the 20th century coined the word "genocide", referred to the Albigensian Crusade, as "one of the most conclusive cases of genocide in religious history (Staff N. , 2014). The Vatican outlawed Sun gazing as Sun worship, and we can assume people who valued their lives discontinued the practice of staring at the Sun.

Pope Innocent III (Latin: Innocentius III; 1160 or 1161 – 16 July 1216) reigned from 8 January 1198 to his death in 1216. His birth name was Ottaviano dei Conti di Segni sometimes anglicised to Lothar of Segni.

If the Vaitican learned of people practicing Sun gazing you were labeled a heretic and murdered. Is it making sense how Sun gazing blotted out of the church? Churches that practiced Sun gazing were rubbed out like a mafia hit in the *Godfather*. Pope Leo the Innocent III

waged a twenty-year campaign to kill the people of Cathar who also practiced Sungazing, and to erase it from the collective conscious.

The Vatican became like the Pharisees condemned by Jesus Himself! The *keys to knowledge* were hidden by the very institution that executed mass murder on those who practiced the righteous path. The Sumerians, Akkadians, Assyrians, and especially ancient Egyptians influenced Judeo-Christian spiritual practices, and the Vatican stamped out spiritual activation. The next Vatican initiative was to hide the Sun in plain view and keep the true properties of it hidden. The Vatican, the origin of the modern church system also carries these

Sumerian, Akkadian, Assyrian, and Babylonia original symbols of the Sun for their classifications of solar symbology on their very altars.

This evidence the Vatican's knowledge of the ancient origin of the Sun's role in our spiritual history and their direct knowledge of the other world, which is the true origin of life on Earth. The Vatican's secret is the Sun's transformative capabilities of the human body by solarizing the pineal gland. There are Vatican churches that place the Sumerian, Akkadian, Assyrian, and Babylonia original symbols of the Sun, prominently on alters. Proving the Vatican's inner knowledge that the Sun is key for spiritual transformation, yet it is hiding in plain view.

If the civilizations of Sumerian, Akkadian, Assyrian, and Babylonia were truly one-hundred percent pagan then why are their symbols displayed and interwoven into the tapestry of Vatican ceremonial wardrobe? If you analyze the symbols on the Vatican's mitre, robes, and sashes you will see variations of Shamash "The Sun God" embroidered on them. The Vatican became the great teacher of spiritual things, yet they hid the one thing for people to flower spiritually. This was done to control the masses and to disconnect them from the other world they were designed to integrate their spiritual selves.

The Essenes were a Jewish mystical sect, and many scholars believe Jesus was one of them. They nested throughout the Judean Desert along the Dead Sea. Scholars debate if they originated in 100 BC and if they are truly the authors of the Dead Sea Scrolls. There is even debate that John the Baptist was part of the Essenes. They most likely fled after Titus destroyed Jerusalem in 70 A.D. The Essenes became deeply connected to the celestial and even stated on one of the

Dead Sea Scrolls, "*there are certain planetary alignments to pray into.*"

In Swami Nirmalananda Giri's article, *The Christ of India* (Giri, 2018), Swami presents research that claims that Jesus Christ was a practicing Sungazer. Sungazing was a common practice in the Essene sect of early Christianity. The Essenes had many practices that were similar to the schools of yoga in India, including:

> *"They believed that the sun was a divine manifestation, imparting spiritual powers to both body and mind. They faced the rising and setting sun and recited prayers of worship, refusing, upon rising in the morning, to speak a single word until the conclusion of those prayers. They did not consider the sun was a god, but a symbol of the One God of Light and Life. It was, though, felt that appropriate prayers directed toward the sun would evoke a divine response."*

We must consider the plausibility of Christ being in India because from age twelve to thirty there is no Scripture of His life. Now in addition to the paintings in this book, you have an account of Christ practicing

Sungazing. There are more accounts about Christ visiting India and an experience with a king of India. I often wonder if the books documenting Jesus's travels to other countries are hidden in Vatican archives? Another ancient Indian book of Kashmiri history, the *Bhavishya Maha Purana* (Yogi, 2008), speaks of an account of the meeting of a king of Kashmir with Jesus, sometime after the middle of the first century:

> *When the king of the Sakas came to the Himalayas, he saw a dignified person of golden complexion wearing a long white robe. Astonished to see this foreigner, he asked, 'Who are you?' The dignified person replied in a pleasant manner: 'Know me as Son of God [Isha Putram], or Born of a Virgin*
>
> *Kumarigarbhasangbhawam.*
>
> *Being given to truth and penances, I preached the Dharma to the mlecchas ... O King, I hail from a land far away, where there is no truth, and evil knows no limits. I appeared in the country of the mlecchas as Isha Masiha [Jesus Messiah] and I suffered at their hands. For I said unto them,*

"Remove all mental and bodily impurities. Remember the Name of our Lord God. Meditate upon Him Whose abode is in the center of the sun."

There in the land of mleccha darkness, I taught to love, truth, and purity of heart. I asked human beings to serve the Lord. But I suffered at the hands of the wicked and the guilty. In truth, O King, all power rests with the Lord, Who is in the center of the sun. And the elements, and the cosmos, and the sun, and God Himself are forever. Perfect, pure, and blissful, God is always in my heart. Thus my Name has been established as Isha Masiha.' After having heard the pious words from the lips of this distinguished person, the king felt peaceful, made obeisance to him, and returned."

Bhavishya Maha Purana 3.2.9-31
(circa 5th century C.E.)

This testimony from Christ where He says, *"Remove all mental and bodily impurities. Remember the Name of our Lord God. Meditate upon Him. Whose abode is in the center of the sun."* The modern church is certainly compliant with teachings to purify ourselves mentally and consistently teaches the message of love. Purifying the body is not a predominant criterion for many churches and many preachers suffer with "pastor body." Meaning most of us do not eat healthy and many people abuse: tobacco, alcohol, and other drugs; legal or illegal.

These are obvious keys to knowledge hidden from the masses through the church system. We are not just to purify our hearts, but our bodies as well. There must be a solar reaction with our emotional and physical bodies as we progressively mature through Sungazing. Next, Christ makes the statement, *"Meditate upon Him. Whose abode is in the center of the sun."* This might sound outlandish, but His statement certainly aligns with the Renaissance paintings in the previous chapter.

Many of the painters captured beings coming out of the Winter Triangle (mostly angels) which is located in Orion and exiting out of the Sun. I am persuaded if our pineal organs became solarized we would see and hear these Wonderful creatures. Because of the Sungazing process is hidden from the masses, people are confounded when Sungazing associates with Christ.

Is it possible the missing years of Christ were removed from the Bible because it was full of Sungazing details?

The quote under the title in this chapter is from the (Lambdin, 1998) Gospel of Thomas. It became discovered in 1945 among a group of books known as the Nag Hammadi library. Biblical scholars reviewed it and it was not included because it did not possess the same literary styles of the other gospels. If you take the time to read it, you will see it does not damage Christ nor contradict the Godhead. It was removed because scholars did not think it was a good fit. What it does give are insights into the mind of Christ and it makes a profound statement regarding the Pharisees.

In the Gospel of Thomas, 39, Jesus said, "*The Pharisees and the scribes have taken the keys of knowledge (gnosis) and hidden them. They themselves have not entered, nor have they allowed to enter those who wish to. You, however, be as wise as serpents and as innocent as doves.*" Two things should stand out here. Firstly, this explains the anger of Christ at the Pharisees because they had taken the "keys of knowledge" and hidden them from the people for spiritual development. They are still hidden today within the church.

Secondarily, Jesus said, "be as wise as serpents and as innocent as doves." Jesus said this very thing in Matthew 10:16, "Behold, I send you forth as sheep in the midst of wolves: *be ye therefore wise as serpents, and harmless as doves*." I say this to emphasize there are commonalities between gospels. I will not debate on the authenticity of this gospel, I will submit it provides another dimension of understanding of the mind of Christ.

I provided a case proving the Pharisees stunted the spiritual growth of the masses over two thousand years ago. The Sanhedrin became a religious institution of half-truths and this tradition is carried on by the Vatican. Alfred Lord Tennyson said, **"A lie which is half a truth is ever the blackest of lies."** By omission the Pharisees became liars and Jesus despised them because He knew they are hiding the keys to spiritual activation. The Pharisees knew if the people ever connected with the Heavenly governance their quasi-political and religious institution would dismantle due to being unnecessary.

The same thing happened to Blockbuster video when Netflix introduced to consumers a superior means of entertainment. The physical VHS cassettes and DVDs became obsolete as invisible data bits streamed directly to television sets. Jesus publicly called out the Pharisees for lying, and as a result, the Pharisees conspired to murder Jesus and pulled out all stops to make it happen. The Pharisees could not risk the people's spiritual transformation.

This would dismantle the people's reliance on the Sanhedrin, and they would no longer be the authority on spiritual guidance. I believe this applies to the Vatican as well. The Renaissance painters made it obvious the Sun is of great spiritual importance, as did the ancients. Is it not ironic that the world searches for extraterrestrial life while the spiritual Universe is teeming with life?

Spiritual communication explains how advanced knowledge passed on to humankind without an alien race physically landing on the Earth. All our perceptions are influenced by the media and most especially by Hollywood. How many of you have seen a movie where aliens attack the Earth? Or the most popular alien movie, E.T.?

Humankind is conditioned to search for sentient life from another physical planet by Hollywood. We have new television shows like "The Orville" where a spaceship warps drives around the Universe serendipitously encountering new life forms. Star Wars and Star Trek are billion-dollar franchises where both perpetuate the fantasy the Universe is teeming with diverse life forms, but scientifically the Earth consistently remains alone and special. This is part of the distraction process. Humans externally seek for proof of external life when Jesus clearly said, "The Kingdom is within."

Activating the Kingdom within is the only way to be included with the Spiritual Kingdom. Right now, modern man relies on Faith as proof the Spiritual Kingdom exists but ancients operated out of *knowing*. In ancient times, they did not rely on just Faith because they spiritually transformed and witnessed the Spiritual Kingdom. The secret ancient knowledge for spiritual transformation was methodically located, then eradicated, and hidden long before the birth of America. The ancient cultures were rooted in the spiritual knowledge while modern man is rooted in technology.

Humankind is now on the cusp of the singularity where artificial intelligence will drive our daily lives. The caveat is artificial intelligence is devoid of a soul and has no mechanism for entrance into the spiritual

Assyrians Represented Sun On A Kite

A kite shape was used to symbolize the Sun hangs in the sky like a kite. This did not represent a flying machine as some scholars suggest.

realm. As the singularity spreads, it guarantees separation from spirit. Artificial intelligence is the antithesis of spiritual intelligence.

Artificial intelligence diminishes critical thought and the technocracy will write the human developmental guidelines of our future. The Sun will shine hoping to capture the attention of the observer, but they will most likely be trained on a smart device. Every two years processing components in computers double in power and with it comes increased performance and new compatibilities.

My point is it will be increasingly difficult to turn people away from technology to "improve" their lives. The modern-day church teaches a half-truth every Sunday by not spelling the proper methodology for spiritual transformation. So far between the Pharisees and the Vatican, the *keys to knowledge* have been hidden. I hope this book changes that!

Hiding the keys of knowledge was an act of self-preservation starting with the Pharisees. Our spirit construct sets us apart from all Creation and makes us special. We have special abilities as we can shift between material and spirit. The material world offers an abundance of pleasures, if you have enough money, we can see why the Pharisees and the Vatican preserved theirs through omission to mass murder.

Academia has humanized almost every aspect of ancient symbols by not seeing spiritual or biological activators embedded in stone. Objectively, observing the winged disc of Ashur you can clearly see the shape of the flying object is very similar to the modern kite. If this was supposed to be a flying machine, the design is certainly inadequate, and at best it could be a hand glider. Just the fact that some in academia ran away with Zacharia Sitchin's assessment this was an extraterrestrial "flying machine" further hid the keys to knowledge in the deepest recesses of the minds of men.

The "keys of knowledge" were hidden for several reasons. Selfish financial reasons and control of the people became the norm. The Vatican used extreme prejudice to eradicate the connection to Sun gazing to Christ if we are to believe the story of the Carthas. Academia and conspiracy theorist are quick to smack an extraterrestrial label on many ancient things, while Spirit is the true originator of all things. The ancients made sure to embody a reoccurring theme in stone edifices, relief walls, and tablets for spiritual transformation.

When is the last time a prosperity preacher advised their flock to Sun gaze? None of them have earned the right to have a Sun disc painted behind their heads. Prosperity preachers guarantee to keep their flock in a state of spiritual atrophy and their own bank accounts bursting. Many prosperity sheep will celebrate Christ when their credit score increases, but they have no idea they possess dormant spiritual powers.

Do you think these prosperity preachers want their flock meditating to Scripture while Sungazing twice a day? Then one day their entire flock's pineal gland becomes active, and the prosperity preacher no longer has tithes coming to their bank account. For the global system to stay intact, the true path must be hidden from the masses.

Filling your heart with love, purifying your body, and Sun gazing will create a new society on Earth. The real secret is what exactly comes out of the Sun and enters the human body? This cannot happen according to the god of this world! Just by reading this book, you will alter your spiritual destiny.

If you practice the examples of Christ and Sun gaze, you will no longer be a part of this world. You will walk in the shoes of the ancients. Christ is called the Prince of Peace, and that is one of the results of Sungazing is peace. Everything you deal with in your life will then be executed from peace and love.

Do you really think the powers-that-be want the motto of the Earth to be, "Peace and Love?" I did not want to spend an exorbitant amount of time on this chapter because most of us can figure out why the keys of knowledge were hidden by the Pharisees and the Vatican. Christ was killed to stop His teachings from flourishing and Jesus demonstrated the conversion process to Spirit.

This explains why almost all the Disciples were murdered. If spiritual transformation was to occur, it would make technology obsolete and the governments of this world obsolete as well. There would be no need for the Vatican as the stewards of spiritual cultivation. We have no idea how long ancient cultures thrived, but many believe ancient Egypt was a dynasty for three thousand years.

Antediluvian cultures probably lasted much than ancient Egypt because they originated closer to the true path. Ancient cultures flourished because the communities practiced spiritual transformation. The side effects of spiritual transformation for humans was peace, love, and harmony. I trust over vast epochs, especially at the end of the Age, a catastrophic global cataclysm destroyed entire civilizations.

The Dark Ages were the harbinger of ignorance, superstition and spiritual death with some notions that are alive today. It is safe to assume many people today holdfast to Dark Age thinking. They walk around full of beliefs with no abilities to demonstrate the Spirit. Because the keys of knowledge are missing it opens the door for the uninitiated to become self-proclaimed religious icons, in their own minds.

This is why there is a cult of personality leading people down religious roads that lead to nowhere. There is a menagerie of self-proclaimed spiritual leaders whose true purpose is profit and not spiritual transformation. The keys of knowledge are immutable, and we need only return to them once discovered. Release the spiritual dead weight in your life and return to the ancients for guidance.

Egyptian Evidence

"The Kingdom of Heaven is within You, and whosoever shall know himself shall find it."

Ancient Egyptian proverb

Where have we heard the above quote from before? Jesus also said this very thing! The ancient Egyptian culture is probably the most investigated out of all ancient cultures. It was invaded by British archeologist, and many spent their entire careers there. It is a blessing the country Egypt stayed intact since ancient time; even the Old Testament prophesied it would still be a nation called Egypt.

If you read, the ancient Egyptian proverb above you will get a sense the Bible has origins in ancient Egypt. Was ancient Egypt always multiple gods worshiping Dynasty? The closer you are to the beginning of the age of humankind, the closer you must be to the truth. I have already shown you how academia has misinterpreted symbols and polluted the wellspring of truth. Have they done the same thing with ancient Egypt?

We are at the mercy of scholars who interject their own opinions, and because we cannot translate, we are at the mercy of their analysis and theories. We now know the Sumerians left us symbols not just pointing to the Sun, but that we should be gazing at it. In turn, the Sun will send something into to us; if we are pure at heart. This something defines as cakes, ale, grail, flowers of life, and finally the dove. Is that not exciting?

Most of us can appreciate the Sun, but ancient knowledge has been suppressed to keep us from communing with the Sun for spiritual cultivation. Revisiting ancient Egypt with solar glasses yields fresh perspectives that will transform our lives on Earth. Everything Christ said we can do we will be able to do! There is another Scripture in the Book of Psalms 82:6, that says, *"I have said, Ye are gods, and all of you are children of the Most High."*

The ancient Egyptians thrived as a culture, and they used the Sun as a transformer to enter the spirit realm. Were the ancient Egyptians worshiping the Sun or using it as a tool? Is academia driving this Sun "worship" narrative? The ancient Egyptians certainly knew the Kingdom within based on the ancient Egyptian proverb. What distinctly stands out about the ancient Egyptian are the tools they used in conjunction with Sungazing.

Bas-relief walls frequently show ancient Egyptians holding an ankh in one hand and a was-scepter in the other. On the bottom of the was-scepter are two prongs that look similar to an electrical prong. The was-scepter is designed to plug into the earth. The ankh and the was scepter were made from copper to conduct extremely low voltage.

For those of you who do not know copper is a common reddish metallic element that is ductile and malleable and one of the best conductors of heat and electricity. I believe the was-scepter was used to ground the person while Sungazing and barefoot on the soil. There are pictures of bas-relief walls with ankhs combined with a djed; which is the ancient Egyptian word for a pillar, but I believe it was an ancient low voltage battery, similar to Tesla coils. If the djeds specifications were like the Baghdad battery, then they generated less than one volt.

I believe ankhs had a modest current flowing through them and this is where things get fascinating. The University of Queensland (Lazaro, 2012) completed a study on melanin and discovered the pigment is a superconductor of electricity and magnetism. *"There are very few examples of natural organic semiconductors and melanin was thought to be the very first example, demonstrated to be such in the early 70s,"* said Professor Meredith. Co-author Associate Professor Powell said, *"We've now found that in melanin, both electrons and ions play important roles."*

Professor Meredith, further added, *"Melanin is able to 'talk' to both electronic and ionic control circuitry and hence can provide that connection role,"* about the study's finding, the culmination of ten years of research and experiments. This is a striking discovery because the ancient Egyptians was a Negroid civilization before it integrated with foreign nationals. Their gods were depicted as jet black, and that would make their skin superconducting! So, these jet-black people would hold low voltage ankhs in one hand and ground themselves with the was scepter, pulling a subtle current from the Earth while being bombarded with ultraviolet radiation.

Melanin – the pigment that colors skin, eyes, and hair could soon be the face of a new generation of biologically friendly electronic devices used in applications such as medical sensors and tissue stimulation treatments.

Led by Professor Paul Meredith and Associate Professor Ben Powell at The University of Queensland, an international team of scientists has published a study that for the first time gives a remarkable insight into the electrical properties of this pigment and its biologically compatible "bioelectronic" features.

The University of Queensland, UQ News, June 27, 2012

Incorporating the copper ankh and was-scepter while Sun gazing sets off a chain reaction through the superconducting skin and I believe activated DNA, and this DNA is not junked DNA, but DNA for activating Spirit. If they were grounded there was no danger in damaging their DNA. Now we can understand the origin of the phrase, "Stay grounded." The ancient Egyptians were aware of the effects of ultraviolet light and frequency on DNA, and therefore they incorporated the low voltage ankh and was-scepter into their Sungazing

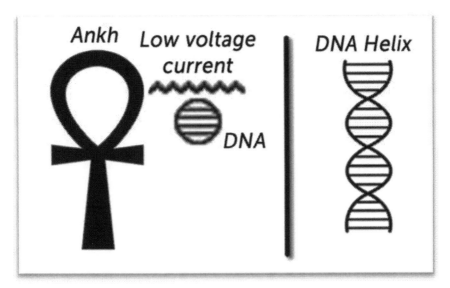

Ancient Egyptian hieroglyphics compared to DNA Helix

routines.

All DNA is distinctly unique, and we do pass down hereditary traits through reproduction. With ancient Egyptian gods, all of them demonstrated unique abilities which I believe was the by-product of their DNA. After successfully Sun gazing with the "rod and staff" a gene switch was hit, and their dormant DNA was activated. I suspect ancient Egyptian Sun-gazers were guided from the Heavenly realm from Sirius through our Sun.

Academia called them Sun worshipers, but I believe they did not worship the Sun but valued it

because they knew it transformed them. The Assyrians left us a wonderful golden nugget with Ashur's tablet and the ancient Egyptians illustrating the spiritual transformation process using copper tools while Sun gazing; and most likely the secret to activating dormant DNA. Based on the University of Queensland study we can deduce electricity and magnetic energy was coursing through their bodies. Perhaps they become magnetized and the Sun shoots the "dove" into their bodies when their hearts are pure? (Sarfati, 2007)

If you look closely at the Assyrian depiction of the Sun when Ashur draws his bow, you will see the origin of the Christian dove at the end of the arrow. You must admit the shape of the arrowhead is remarkably similar to the dove. This reminds me of the spectacle when T.D. Jakes was on the altar, and Tyler Perry laid hands on him, and he began to "house quake" suggesting the Holy Spirit was involved. Now we know the Holy Spirit or dove is something that comes out of the Sun based on the ancient origin.

The Holy Spirit depicts as a "dove" that shoots out of the Sun and enters those pure of heart who follow the path Jesus demonstrated to His Disciples. The spectacle performed by T.D. Jakes and Tyler Perry that Sunday on the megachurch alter did not include the Holy Spirit. Now you see the ancient origin of the Holy Spirit dove and the fact some of these pastors are entertainers.

Receiving the Holy Spirit is a direct result of being purified, full of love, Sungazing and the Sun reciprocating. What is the point of Joel Osteen, Creflo Dollar, Jim Bakker, and so-called spiritual leaders of this ilk? Including the many other prosperity preachers who have never had their day in the Sun? The filthy rich prosperity preachers teach a feel-good message to their followers, but as you can see, none of them will ever be spiritually transformed.

Now we understand Matthew 19:24, where Jesus said, *"And again I say unto you, it is easier for a camel to go through the eye of a needle, than for a rich man to enter into the kingdom of God."* These prosperity preachers are so distracted by their wealth they do not even seek the Kingdom within, nor can they demonstrate one thing the Disciples demonstrated. How to gain access to the Kingdom within is not included in the prosperity Gospel because it is more concerned with money. The Kingdom within will never be obtained with the prosperity gospel.

Jesus did not come to Earth to improve our credit scores, but to demonstrate the power of the Spirit. We are so critical of these ancient cultures, but they were thoughtful enough to leave us artifacts showing us the most important celestial object in the sky. The ancients knew by returning to the ancient ways we would receive the knowledge we need from the Heavenly realms. The ancient Egyptians left clearer clues how to activate our dormant DNA by using the Sun.

This is why ancient Egypt had so many people perceived as gods especially when observed by non-Sun gazing witnesses. The Sumerian hero, Sun god Shamash, and messiah carried a ring and a staff and iterations of these apparatus were passed along to subsequent civilizations. This should negate the alien agenda and show us how the wonders of the world were constructed. The Sun provided a gateway for consultation from Heavenly beings located in Orion ruled by the Most High and His Son.

This also explains why the ancient Egyptians carried on the practice of aligning key architecture with Orion. Angels illustrated in paintings from the Vatican reformation include the Sirius star. In fact, the Sirius star system is part of the Winter Triangle, and the ancient Egyptians revered the star, Sirius. When it comes to the birth of Creation, many ancient cultures all refer to Orion.

Christianity is no different in this sense. The triangle is a prominent feature in Vatican art, and I believe it represented the gateway to a world of spiritual beings, including the choirs of angels. I previously shared art by Athanasius Kircher, who was a Jesuit scholar who prominently featured the Winter triangle constellation in his artwork. Kircher established a connection between the Winter Triangle, Sirius and our Sun. The Sirius star was the portal to Heavenly beings and they had an intimate relationship with humankind.

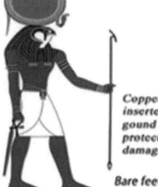

Ancient Egyptian Method of Sun gazing to activate dormant DNA

The Sun is the mechanism for transformation and the snake is the DNA.

Melinated skin becomes superconducting of electricity and magnetism.

The copper ankh has a low voltage current. Powered by the djed (battery).

Copper was-scepter is inserted into the earth to gound the person. This protected the DNA from damage.

Bare feet grounded on the Earth

They would counsel the kings of the Earth, which also explains why advanced ancient architecture arrived on the Earth. Evidence of this is the precision stone cutting tools, and the transportation of giant megaliths, which modern technology is unable to duplicate, nor cranes lift. Do you not see the correlation between the Vatican and the ancient Egyptians when it comes to gods and angels? The ancient cultures practiced a methodology of spiritual cultivation where masters, prophets, and the Son of God manifest to retrain humankind.

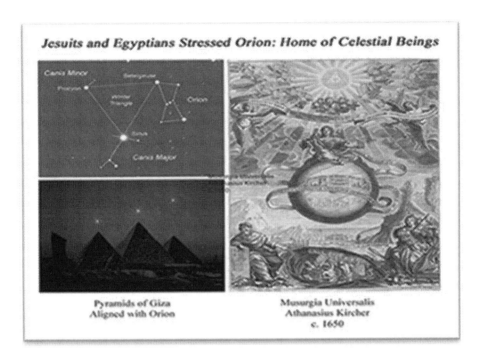

The Winter Triangle is a prominent feature in religious art and represents the Winter Triangle constellation. Aerial views of ancient Egyptian topography revealed the Pyramids of Giza are a representation of the Orion Constellation. Two distinctly different civilizations point to Orion as the home of Celestial Beings connected to the Earth

This was a common theme of bridging the material and spirit worlds over vast epochs. We now live in a society where people are discouraged from direct sunlight. The windows to the soul are the eyes, yet tinted lenses block the light. The workweek is designed to drive the masses away from safe sunrise during rush hour.

There is no time to gaze at the sunset, the speed of living this life made sure of that. This is a system designed to divorce the Sun from our collective conscious as the DNA spiritual activator in our lives. Yet, the ancients embedded the Sun, pineal gland, and DNA in stone . . . so humans will never forget. Vilifying the ancient Egyptians guaranteed many Christians not explore what made them a spiritual Dynasty.

There are many bas-reliefs and hieroglyphics of various humans holding the ankh and was-scepter. There is documented evidence pharaohs and gods carried the ankh and was-scepter. European scholars claimed the ankh and was-scepter were just symbols of power for royalty. We cannot blame the material-minded for their failure in identifying spiritual tools.

Without the proper context, academia once mistakenly labeled the Assyrian symbol for the Sun as a "rocket ship." George Orwell, said, "Who controls the past controls the future. Who controls the present controls the past." Have you noticed most of the world has abandoned the spiritual path and now consumed by technology?

I believe this was by design to thwart our collective duality as material and spiritual beings. Instead of using spiritual telepathy we text message where technology replaces our spiritual abilities. When ancient Egypt originally drew academics, many were White Supremacist who suppressed melanated corpses. Numerous eighteenth-century scholastic stories are driven by assumptions, predisposition, preference, and prejudice. Even today, many scholars believe the Sun was just an emblem to ancient Egyptians.

Sometimes you cannot see the forest for the trees. We are living in the Information Age and knowledge is shared at a higher speed. Many people are intuitively investigating ancient ways in the hopes of duplicating the miracles of Jesus. Many have overlooked Jesus said, "Follow my ways..." yet, they bastardize politics, end times, fear porn, and prosperity, with His teachings for spiritual transformation.

Jesus came to *demonstrate* what we can all do *if* we follow His ways. This implies considering and doing as He did and not any other person in the Bible. At face value, we should all realize it is time to return to the Sun as a tool for spiritual cultivation. It would appear melanin has role for sleeping DNA activation. It also explains why highly melanated cultures reigned for thousands of years and maybe is the reason dark skinned cultures are despised.

The high-level ancient Egyptian gods are most likely explanations for Creation forces, the building blocks of Nature, and other scientific forces we understand today. In my opinion, many of the other ancient gods were humans who graduated the Sungazing process. We have seen Renaissance art illustrate this very thing with the halo disc behind the head of prominent people in the Bible. They were the examples of what the human could be when physical beings activate their spiritual minds.

We should all revisit ancient Egypt wearing solar glasses and see this was a civilization based on Sungazing. It should be obvious the Sumerians passed their understanding of the Sun to subsequent civilizations. We can now see the obelisk in a new light and I submit they were giant sundials. This way the entire population would know when to Sun gaze as a community safely.

The obelisk later became phallic symbols and then called pagan symbols to dissuade people from rediscovering ancient ways. This reminds me of Pope

Innocent III, labeling Cathar citizens, heretics and launching a twenty-year genocide on the people, a people who are said to have incorporated Sun gazing with their walk with Christ. Sir Ernest Alfred Thompson Wallis Budge (27 July 1857 – 23 November 1934) was an English Egyptologist, Orientalist, and philologist who worked for the British Museum and published numerous works on the ancient Near East. He made numerous trips to Egypt and Sudan on behalf of the British Museum to buy antiquities and helped it build its collection of cuneiform tablets, manuscripts, and papyri.

He published many books on Egyptology, helping to bring the findings to larger audiences. In 1920, Ernest Alfred Thompson Wallis Budge was knighted for his administration to Egyptology and the British Museum. One of his works was his translation of the "Papyrus of Ani" which he dubbed, "The Egyptian Book of the Dead." I believe this is the wrong name for the "Papyrus of Ani."

It ought to be called, "The Egyptian Book of the Other World" and calling it the "Book of the Dead" is misleading and I accept as off base. Additionally, I believe it is the Kingdom from whence Christ came. Let us continue with an excerpt to gain more insight:

> *Hail, O ye who give cakes and ale to perfect souls in the House of Osiris, give ye cakes and ale twice each day (in the morning and in the evening) to the soul of the Osiris Ani, whose word is true before the gods, the Lords of Abydos, and whose word is true with you.*
> (Budge, 1240 BC)

A reference to "morning and night" is identified with the dawn and dusk. What is fascinating is the Sun giving "cakes and ale" to perfect souls. This speaks to the condition of the heart Jesus preached about. Jesus always instructed us to love one another and stay in a state of love, without sin.

Next, there is a "food" and "drink" component associated with Sungazing. Is it a coincidence "ale" sounds strikingly similar to "grail?" If you were a rapper this would not be a crime to create a flow with those exchangeable words. I think the terms "cake" and "ale" denote pleasure to illustrate Sun gazing will make you feel good.

Ecclesiastes 11:7 makes a remarkably similar statement with, "Truly, the light is sweet, and a pleasant thing it is for the eyes to behold the sun." Is the Holy Grail something we can get from the Sun when we Sun look before it with culminated hearts? "Cake" is additionally an interesting food association for solar nourishment since the cake is tasty and causes great pleasure to brain receptors. How many people do you know that hate cake? I think the "cake" impact make the human body feel satisfied and satisfied.

If we revisit religious art, we will see a connection with the Holy Grail (ale) and a solar delivery system. Here we can see the association with the Sun and furthermore the fire lit and consume from the highest point of the blessed messengers head. This symbolizes the sun-powered initiation of the pineal organ. At long last, the holy messenger is holding the Holy Grail which is the thing that the ideal soul will get from the Sun.

The old Egyptians knew about a sun-based law then when legitimately presented to the Sun a reward framework initiated. At this point in our ancient understanding, three things emanate from the Sun. The first would be the "cake" and "ale" which are the pleasure sensations in the human body and the Holy

Spirit dove, which shoots out of the Sun into the human body. This lets us know there is a conceivable deliberate impact on the human body.

The dove from the Sun shooting into the human body is the final state every Sungazer is seeking. I trust this is the powerful pilot light that shows in the pineal organ, which thus actuates the otherworldly DNA we know as Spirit. The "cake and ale" are the sunlight-based compound impacts, which satisfies the brains joy receptors. Ale must have chosen as the symbol because of the euphoria over the entire human body.

The Egyptian Book of the Dead then goes on to describe another world and Jesus referred to this world. In John 8:23, Jesus says, "*And he said unto them, Ye are from beneath; I am from above: ye are of this world; I am not of this world.*" In the earlier presented religious paintings, you see two worlds represented. The spiritual world is spoken to by the triangle gateway, which I accept speaks to the Sirius star in the Winter Triangle.

This world is sometimes painted teeming with Beings, so we can deduce it is heavily populated. We know Sirius is a star in the Winter Triangle, even the

The Angel of the Holy Grail
Ernest W Twining
c. 1935

Dogon Tribe in Africa is associated with Sirius, and ancient Egypt's Pyramids of Giza are lined up with the Sirius star. The ancient Egyptians were in communication with beings in Orion via spirit and "The Egyptian Book of the Dead" outlined rules to engage with this world. We can still do this today if we return to the ancient spiritual-biological transformation process.

Not to worship the Sun but rather to utilize it as the Heavenly partner of Jesus. I trust the snake on the head dressings of the ancient Egyptians spoke to the activation of the pineal gland, and torpid DNA was awakened. They had a small Sun ignited in their brains that activated the duality of the design of man. Now, our spirit bodies are sleeping until they are awoken and supported by water, Sungazing, fasting, and petition by prayer.

The primary keys are given by Jesus and that is to love each other while striving not to sin. Love is an impression of an immaculate soul and draws the "Sacred Spirit" into the human body, in conjunction with water, Sungazing, fasting, and petition of prayer. I cannot stress this profound initiation process enough since everything must be done all together for the Holy dove to shoot out of the Sun and enter the human body. Any sin manifest in the human soul will negate the solar exchange process. You will receive some of the benefits the Sun has to offer, such as mood elevation, circadian rhythm normalization, and endocrine regulation.

Why would ancient cultures like the Assyrians go through so much trouble to embody the Sun, pineal gland, and DNA in stone? I believe they did this, so humans would never forget the recipe for spiritual self-actuation. There also must be a utility to the Holy Land in relation to the Sun. There are consistent Biblical stories of prominent Biblical characters climbing mountains and mystical experience.

I wonder if it is necessary to get as close to the Sun as possible for conditioning and to one day receive the Holy Spirit? This is part of the detective work which is necessary for our spiritual actuation. Mount Hermon is a mountain cluster constituting the southern end of the Anti-Lebanon mountain range. Its highest peak is 9230 feet and the highest point inside Israel's borders today is Mizpe Shelagim at 7295 feet.

I often wonder if approximation to the Sun is of vital importance and this one of the reasons Mount Hermon was considered sacred land. Mount Hermon is certainly not the world's tallest mountain, but many major Biblical moments happened there. According to the Book of Enoch, Mount Hermon, is where the 200 "fallen" angels descended and taught the world how to live in its current ill state. I am not sure if mountain elevation is a requirement to Sun Gazing.

When Jesus went on his forty days fast He traveled to the Judean Desert. The Judaean Desert is an array of hills and canyons, falling from the heights of around 1,000 meters in the Judean Mountain. I believe He went there not just for solitude, but because the mountain elevation brought Him closer to the Sun. There must be a connection between elevation and Sun gazing with the goal of spiritual transformation.

DNA, Glands, and Sunlight

"We are spiritual beings whether we want to admit it or not, and inherent in our DNA is a design to return us home - home to our true essence, our greatest self, our limitless self." -

Debbie Ford

When you experience truth, you ought to praise it and the above statement is a festival of a significant truth for humankind. In fact, it is profound, and it perfectly explains the genetic design of the human body. We are designed to experience two distinctly unique worlds! This might sound ridiculous, but ancient accounts testify to this very thing. We do know from ancient testimony Jesus returned to His Father's Kingdom, but Enoch and Elijah are examples of humans who traveled between worlds.

Enoch and Elijah left the material plane and crossed to the otherworldly kingdom. I believe their fully activated DNA allowed them to do this. Numerous individuals have encountered near-death (Mary Neal, 2017) and numerous can acknowledge the believability the spirit has made a trip to the Heavenly domain, after the experience. The question is what are the variables and catalyst that make this possible? Those answers are locked tight in our human DNA.

> *Today's scientists have come to a similarly dichotomous recognition that exposure to the ultraviolet radiation (UVR) in sunlight has both beneficial and deleterious effects on human health. Sunburn is caused by too much UVB radiation; this form also leads to direct DNA damage and promotes various skin cancers.* (Mead, 2008)
> *US National Library of Medicine, National Institutes of Health, Benefits of Sunlight: A Bright Spot for Human Health - M. Nathaniel Mead*

This means exposure to the Sun at high noon is detrimental to some skin. It certainly does not explain the African experience to excessive amounts of sunlight without a high population of skin cancer. The best-known benefit of sunlight is its ability to boost the body's vitamin D supply, most cases of vitamin D deficiency are due to lack of outdoor sun exposure. Vitamin D is a steroid hormone that specifically impacts more than 200 out of nearly 20,000 to 25,000 human protein-coding qualities and strikingly ties to various qualities related to an immune system illness and tumor.

There is a chemical reaction when the Sun bathes the human body in ultraviolet radiation. One of the many benefits of Sungazing is the promotion of overall health. In fact, science will learn that safe sunlight balances the chemical secretions of the endocrine system. Is it possible this world would be cancer free if all people Sun gazed? There are also medical journals reporting people who are further away from the equator have higher rates of multiple sclerosis. (Davis, 2016)

These two medical findings suggest that safe sunlight (and as "The Egyptian Book of the Dead" stated at "sunrise" and "sunset") provide the DNA of the human body the ability to sustain healthy DNA and aid in the DNA repair process. Is anyone surprised some tumors are turned around with the guide of Sun infused herbs? DNA is responsible for how proteins in the human body express themselves and damaged DNA encodes faulty proteins, which when replicated cause disease. Science will find that in addition to a healthy diet sunlight is the great sustainer of DNA normalcy.

The daylight we see is called white light that comprises a segment of hues, most are familiar with these hues split as white light beams through a prism. Daylight is something other than just white light and I trust each shading range has an immediate match to organs of the endocrine framework. When sunlight passed through a prism (there is the triangle again) sunlight segments into component colors: red, orange, yellow, green, blue, and violet. There is a correlation between light and the endocrine system of the human body.

The Sun bombards the Earth with electromagnetic radiation. The Sun also emits X-rays, ultraviolet, visible light, infrared, and even radio waves. The magnetic field and ozone layer of the Earth protect the Earth from harmful levels of radiation. Red and infrared light (600-1000nm) help metabolism in the body on a few distinct levels, correspondingly to supplementing thyroid hormones yet in addition reciprocal to it. Studies show that beaming red light (Half, 2017) directly to the thyroid gland (front of the neck) improves production of the hormones.

When you Sun gaze, your head is raised, and your thyroid is showered in the daylight. Again, we have another example of a gland organ which chemical process initiates by sunlight. Let us circle back to Vitamin D to understand the correlation between hormonal excretions by glands initiated by sunlight. The parathyroid glands are endocrine glands located in your neck close to the thyroid glands.

They secrete the parathyroid hormone which regulates serum calcium and phosphate, which in return regulate the parathyroid hormone. The kidneys metabolize Vitamin D, which is called, 1,25-dihydroxy, and it is the most potent Vitamin D metabolite. How much Vitamin D is produced depends on the amount of the parathyroid hormone and the calcium levels in the body. If calcium is low the body depletes it from the bones.

The lack of sunlight leads to a chain of event in the human body causing imbalance and disease. Foods rich in solar energy are the best choice in conjunction with Sungazing. All of the glands of the human body respond to sunlight and this reminds me of a short-lived Japanese childhood show called (July 17, 1966 – April 9, 1967) *Ultraman*. The main character, Shin Hayata, was a senior member of the Scientific Special Search Party

(SSSP) who was involved in a crash at Ryumagori. The crash bonded him with the hero, Ultraman.

This was a time in television when you could see the wires making the monsters fly and the zipper in the back of the suit. Ultraman's victory never assured, as Ultraman's powers and, indeed, his very life force, came from solar energy, which reduced by Earth's filtering atmosphere. His time limit stated to be three minutes for battle before he needed direct sunlight to recharge, though certain scenes do show him capable of still fighting while exceeding this limit. Looking back, it makes sense his health was driven by the Sun and when his solar energy became depleted the light on his chest began blinking as a warning.

Another interesting correlation is Ultraman hails from Nebula M78. The nebula Messier 78 (also known as M 78 or NGC 2068) is a reflection nebula in the constellation Orion. Nebula M78 discovered by Pierre Méchain in 1780 and included by Charles Messier in his catalog of comet-like objects that same year. Another reference to the Sun and Orion incorporated into fiction, yet with an authentically researched past.

Finally, Ultraman, speaks to the duality of the creation of man. Where a material man lives on the

Earth, but his true origin is somewhere in Orion. I say these things to present the case that sunlight is the therapy our DNA requires to maintain optimal health but also to trigger our DNA to release the hormones necessary to regulate a subtle dormant DNA transformation to Spirit. As previously stated the pineal gland is not the only gland in the human body modulated by sunlight. The major glands that make up the human endocrine system include the: adrenal glands, hypothalamus, pancreas, parathyroid, pineal gland, pituitary glands, reproductive glands, and the thyroid.

The adrenal glands (also known as suprarenal glands) are endocrine glands that produce a variety of hormones including adrenaline and the steroids aldosterone and cortisol. They are found above the kidneys. Each gland has an outer cortex, which produces steroid hormones and an inner medulla. The finding that bright light exposure reduced cortisol levels on the descending phase of the cortisol rhythm suggests that exposure to morning sunlight may have a greater effect on adrenal cortex physiology than previously recognized. (Lam, 2014)

The hypothalamus is an organ in the forebrain underneath the thalamus that directions both the autonomic sensory system and the movement of the pituitary, controlling body temperature, thirst, hunger, and other homeostatic frameworks, and engaged with rest and emotional action. Photosensitive cells in the eye specifically influence the cerebrum's hypothalamus locale, which controls our natural clock. This affects our circadian beat, not only essential for jet lag but rather for typical rest designs, hormone control, expanded response time, and conduct.

The human eye contains photosensitive cells in its retina, with connections directly to the pituitary gland in the brain. Stimulation of these important cells comes from sunlight, in particular, the blue unseen spectrum. A study by Dr.'s Turner and Mainster of the University of Kansas School of Medicine, published in the British Journal of Ophthalmology in 2008 states that, "these photoreceptors play a vital role in human physiology and health." The effects are not only in the brain but in the whole body. (Maffetone P. , 2012)

The pancreas is a gland, situated near the stomach, that secretes a digestive fluid into the intestine through one or more ducts and also secretes the hormone insulin. An Australian study demonstrated that exposure to sunlight protects against cancer of the pancreas. The study made by the researcher Rachel Nyali, from the Institute of Queensland Medical Research, in Australia, that the risk of pancreatic cancer decreased in people who have a history of cancer, skin as well as those born in areas with a high level of UV radiation or persons who are allergic to the sun. (Gadala, 2012)

The parathyroid gland regulates calcium, located behind the thyroid gland in the neck. The parathyroid gland secretes a hormone called parathormone (or parathyrin) that is critical to calcium and phosphorus metabolism. I have already submitted the relationship to Vitamin D production and the parathyroid glands secreting a hormone with sunlight as the catalyst. The pineal gland is the most storied gland in the human body.

René Descartes (1596-1615), French philosopher, mathematician, and scientist, believed the pineal gland to be the "principal seat of the soul". The pineal organ, otherwise called the conarium or epiphysis cerebri, is a little endocrine organ in the vertebrate brain. The pineal organ produces melatonin, a serotonin determined hormone, which adjusts rest designs in both circadian and occasional cycles. The mind's pineal organ benefits straightforwardly from sunlight-based incitement.

In well-evolved creatures, including people, the organ has lost direct photosensitivity, yet reacts to light using a multisynaptic pathway that incorporates a subset of retinal ganglion cells containing the newfound photopigment, melanopsin. Translated this means humans must absorb sunlight through the eyes to activate the pineal gland. The pituitary gland is a pea-sized body attached to the base of the brain; the pituitary is important in controlling growth and development and the functioning of the other endocrine glands. In 1932, Dr. Wendell Krieg, professor of anatomy at Northwestern University, concluded that lack of specific wavelengths of light causes a biochemical or a hormonal deficiency in both plants and animal cells.

He referred to that as a condition of "mal-illumination" similar to malnutrition. In 1969 Dr. Joseph Meites of Michigan State University stated that "light entering the eyes causes nerve impulses that influence the brain and pituitary gland that trigger the release of other hormones". Further stating, *"We have no idea how many diseases are linked with hormone problems, but we do know that several diseases such as diabetes, infertility, cancer, and thyroid disorders are involved with hormonal imbalances.*" What the medical community seems to be missing is *safe* sunlight is not just healthy, but necessary to maintain optimal hormonal balances in the human body.

The times for safe sunlight is one hour after sunrise and one hour before sunset; photographers call this the "golden hours" for the best lighting for outdoor pictures. During safe Sun hours, the Sun will not harm the human endocrine system nor optics of the eye. When sunlight is safely absorbed through the skin and eyes, it causes a chained reaction to the endocrine system. (Maffetone D. P., 2015) It is very similar to the term "daisy-chained" in the technology industry which is defined as, "connect (several devices) together in a linear series."

This why an administrator can control all of the devices from one administrative console. Finally, the regenerative organs, the gonad, sex organ, or conceptive organ is a blended organ that delivers the gametes (sex cells) and sex hormones of a living being. In the female of the species, the regenerative cells are the egg cells, and in the male, the conceptive cells are the sperm. The pineal gland regulates the reproductive glands, and yet again we return to sunlight as the great sustainer of balance in the human body.

Science will one day conclude the full spectrum of white light separated by color component corresponds with a specific gland in the human body. Once the endocrine system is regulated, and the glands are secreting in harmony it will place less stress on the pineal gland, and it will begin to absorb more sunlight. Eventually, it will reach a point where it will illuminate. Photoreceptors convert sunlight, and this sunlight modulates the endocrine system.

Photoreceptive proteins in the cell absorb photons initiating change throughout the human body. I hope I have successfully presented how the human body's endocrine system is designed to be optimized by sunlight. The medical community is learning more each decade on how safe sunlight avoids disease. While religious institutions have yet to embrace the power of the Sun for spiritual cultivation, especially Christianity.

In the early 1990s the term "junk DNA" was introduced to the world through the work of geneticist. Junk DNA is defined as segments of DNA that have no apparent genetic function. The scientific community perpetuated this erroneous understanding of DNA for almost two decades. This junk DNA theory calculated the ninety-seven percent of its three-point-two billion bases had no apparent function.

Now scientists have backtracked and are removing "junk DNA" from their lexicon. They now believe that nine to eighty percent of DNA is operational. What this tells me is these scientists still do not understand one hundred percent of our DNA. We have already grown accustomed to living in a society that is not living in harmony with the Sun.

The average morning for a person consists of getting to work on time. This means there is no habit to Sun gaze safely after Sunrise. Getting home from work is equally challenging and people miss the sunset. Is our DNA dormant because our endocrine system is out of whack? The further we travel back to the known history of the Earth we learn science was included in ancient artifacts.

Even the symbol for DNA strands is embedded in their ancient artifacts. While modern science does not believe ancient cultures understood genetics the Book of Jasher tells a different story. The Bible references the

Book of Jasher several times. What does it have to say about the ancient understanding of genetics?

The ancient Book of Jasher address genetic engineering when it says, "*and the sons of men in those days took from the cattle of the earth, the beasts of the field and the fowls of the air and taught the mixture of animals of one species with the other, in order therewith to provoke the Lord.*" (Jasher 9:18)

This understanding expands to the micro-level where ancient electron microscopes were required to observe the smallest matter. When it comes to the modern man, there is a proclivity for arrogance when it comes to assessing the abilities of the earliest civilizations. Modern humans believe they dwarf ancient cultures in areas such as mathematics, politics, science, art, writing, and architecture, etc. The irony is modern technology cannot replicate ancient architectural wonders.

Modern men have witnessed no powerful men like the *little Sun* known as Sampson. We have no spiritual men who can do one thing Jesus, the Disciples, or the prophets of the Bible were able to demonstrate. This leads me to the next ancient genetic reference through their art. It shows a clear similarity to a strand of DNA and next to it, you will see the ankh. Again, there is an ancient suggestion the ankh is involved with DNA.

Is this the "key" to initiating change to DNA? This combination of the Sun, the ankh, and DNA must be the bridge to the other world. Below is the Sumerian gods Enki and we can safely assume Enki was not accessorizing his outfit with snakes. The snakes look like a strand of DNA!

This Sumerian image relates to genetic strands of DNA. Adapa, was a Sumerian mythical who I believe was a metaphor for DNA, but academics believe Adapa unknowingly refused the gift of immortality. The ankh loans belief again to its relationship to DNA actuation as an apparatus for otherworldly change. You must agree Adapa and DNA are remarkably similar in design.

Additionally, the Sumerian ankh is the mother to the ancient Egyptian ankh; as well as the Ethiopian cross. The Sumerian's embedded a formula in stone so it would never be forgotten. I believe it was a formula for the transformation of man to a spirit body. I believe Jesus was the last representative of this other world to preach about the process and somewhere within the last two thousand years it was hidden.

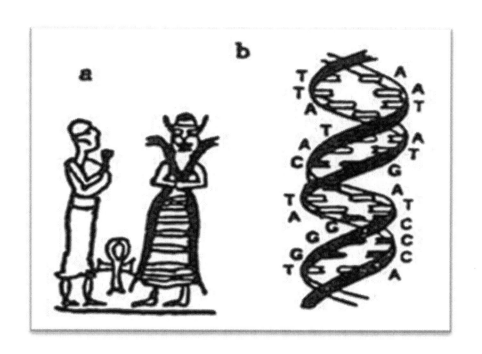

Image of Sumerian's Enki and Adapa

What makes Jesus' voyage to our world stunning is He is royalty and behaved as such. Symbols were renamed, and meanings were changed so even when people see artifacts from the ancient past the meanings would stay hidden. Again, we see the ancient symbol for DNA, and it tells a story. At the top, we see the Sun disc, and then we see the pineal gland and wings denoting an action or even arrival.

Every synonym for the word "flight" can be wrapped up as changing from one place to another. The flight takes you from point A to point B or to different places. Now it makes sense when, Jesus, said, in John 14:6, *"Jesus saith unto him, I am the way, the truth, and the life: no man cometh unto the Father, but by me."* The church system got us halfway there but left out the solar transformation piece.

The Book of Proverbs is the best guide to life I have read, but evidence shows King Solomon was merely carrying on the writings of the ancient Egyptians. Yet, ancient Egypt is vilified in Christian circles, and we are trained to dismiss ancient Egypt before investigating their spiritual customs or methodologies for actuation. The ancients were not just aware of DNA they knew how to change it! There are ancient artifacts peppering museums seething in silence to be noticed.

Let's think about the logic behind the visit from Jesus. He wanted people to follow His ways, so they could connect with the Kingdom while on Earth. Jesus made it unmistakable any power he showed was drawn from the otherworldly kingdom, while in human form. He demonstrated on many occasions the power from this Kingdom while alive in human form, before and after He was resurrected. This is not "make belief," and God isn't a man in the sky of the Earth's atmosphere.

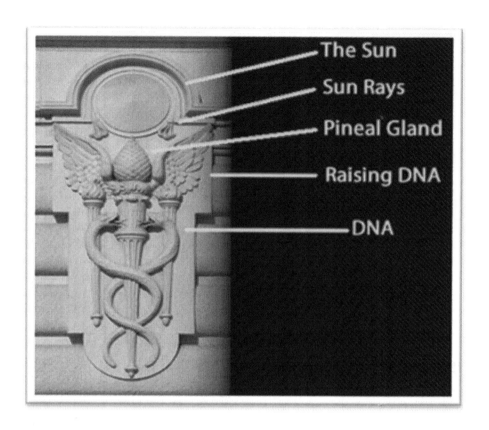

The Sun

Sun Rays

Pineal Gland

Raising DNA

DNA

From all ancient evidence and religious paintings, His Kingdom is somewhere in Orion and most likely near the Sirius star, or maybe even inside the star! We are cut off from this world because our DNA has yet to be purified, spiritualized, or solarized and the ancients left us the clues to implement this change within ourselves. Modern man associates the intertwined snakes with medicine, but that is a half-truth. The ancient intertwined snakes were designed to represent the DNA strand.

Does it not make sense these ancient cultures would prominently acknowledge DNA since they knew how to upgrade it? Or do you believe the ancients were celebrating medicine? The ancients passed on symbols that included a "pine cone" and a "tree of life." Both these symbols have a *physiological match* in the human brain.

They both must be critical to contacting the Heavenly realm and serve another purpose than just material sensing. We first must be able to connect with this other world, and then we must be able to sense the life in the other world. The ancients had this knowledge passed on to them somehow, and it had to be from the Creator. How else would have humankind learned about the invisible?

The "pine cone" matches the shape of the pineal gland in the human brain. It activates by sunlight and regulates other glands in the endocrine system. The ancient symbol for the "tree of life" also matches an area in the brain (Arbor vitae (anatomy), 2005) responsible for transmitting sensory and motor function to the cerebellum in the brain. Sensory functions defines as the extent to which an

"Tree of Life" in the human brain; aka, Arborvitae section of the cerebellum. Its function is to transmit sensory and motor information to and from the cerebellum.

individual correctly senses skin stimulation, sounds, proprioception, taste and smell, and visual images.

The pineal gland does not control the senses so the "tree of life" section of the brain must be transformed to sense the life in the Heavenly realm. What are the chances the human brain would have a component that remarkably resembles the "tree of life" and acts as a transmitter for sensing functions? We also see the

The "King" is holding a staff touching the "tree of life", then pointing at the Sun. The pineal gland is placed in the scene to emphasize the importance of it. This is the ancient formula to raise the signal in the "tree of life."

Assyrian Ashur shooting the Holy Spirit (dove) out of the Sun to show how the "tree of life" transforms.

There must be a relation to a DNA transformation causing new sensory abilities in the "tree of life" part of the cerebellum. What are the chances the storied "tree of life" in Jewish mysticism and the Bible would have a biological representative inside the human brain? Why are we seeing ancient Egyptian symbols associated with

- 138 -

the DNA carved into stone next to the ankh? This must be a "recipe" for transformation that is directly related to the: Sun, ankh, was scepter, and the "tree of life" which lead to Sirius.

This must be the home of our souls and amazingly we can interact with our home world! The ancients left the world timeless stone illustrations, so the conversion power of the Sun would not be overlooked. Hollywood has people believing these are stargates! In truth these illustrations depict the Sun's transformation of the "tree of life" in the human brain raising the signal to its highest. The Sumerians celebrated the minds transition into the Spirit Realm!

Notice the hand on the right holding the pineal gland. I believe these ancient cultures realized when science matured enough we would understand the associations they embedded in stone. This is science and not transport machines for aliens. This is how the ancient would spiritually transform, and this knowledge was passed down to subsequent cultures.

At certain points in history powerful religious institutions located this knowledge and took ownership of it through mass murder. The ancient Egyptians left images to tell the story by capturing advance science like genetics, celestial markers, energy signatures, and apparatus. These are things that would always be identifiable over vast epochs because in most cases they are immutable. There is a connection between the "key of life" and the "tree of life." A key is used to initiate a sequence to start a process.

Doors, safes, and locks are opened with keys. Some processes are started using a "key" and raising your signal in the sensory part of brain's "tree of life" begins using the copper ankh and was-scepter ("rod and staff"), Sungazing and solar pineal gland maturation. The "tree of life" is a universal symbol which has roots in the material and branches out into the ether. The classical definition of a tree is a common universal, archetypal symbol that can be found in many different traditions around the ancient world.

Trees are symbols of physical and spiritual nourishment, transformation and liberation, sustenance, spiritual growth, union, and fertility. The low voltage ankh must, and Sun participates in unlocking of DNA and starting the "tree of life" maturation process. This leads to communion with the Heavenly realm and leads directly to the Most High. The question is: *Did the ancient world truly celebrate the transformation of human DNA or were they worshiping serpents?*

This serpent DNA theme transits through many ancient cultures and not just the: Sumerian, Akkadian, Assyrian, Babylonian, Phoenicians, Egyptians, or Chaldeans, etc. It is apparent the ancients had a mechanism for seeing inside the body at a molecular level. Modern science requires an electron microscope to see DNA. The diameter of a DNA molecule is about 2 nanometers.

A nanometer is one billionth of a meter. Let that sink in for a moment! We can now see in 4,000 BC the ancient civilizations either had the technology, spiritual abilities or received teaching on the DNA encoding of the human body. This would link us to the Winter Triangle of Sirius as the home of the Super Being and beings that participated in the birth of mankind. Next, I present an ancient Egyptian artifact and attempt to tell the story on the left column of the ankh tablet.

Mind you I did not study hieroglyphics at an accredited institution, but I believe the symbols were designed to tell a story which would be decipherable by truth detectives. In my opinion, the left column is telling a story of the Sun radiating down to man altering his

DNA. It shows to the process of Sun gazing with the staff which activates sleep state DNA. We have seen the "half-dome" symbol in the prior religious paintings as the location of the Most High and heavenly beings.

Next, we see an energy signature relating to the staff which prepares the soul for transport. The Sun fuels the connection while physical body Sun gazes and the spiritual body is transported to Sirius. Please note how the second to the last hieroglyph in the left column raises its hands to receive spirit as people do in church today. The "key of life" initiates this entire process.

I believe the right side of the ankh tablet are the procedures on how to return. I could be wrong about this, but intuitively it makes sense to me! I just cannot rely on the European consensus based on their history of prejudice, omissions, and hate toward dark-skinned ancient Egypt. Now when we see images travel through space in a "boat" it starts to make sense. This was not a representation of a physical body in space, but a spiritual body.

Our DNA is designed to experience both worlds at once. Jesus surely demonstrated this as did other major prophets in the Torah. This is how the Most High made

us . . . special! Can you imagine your soul transporting to Orion and experiencing the Kingdom of the Most High and then returning to Earth?

There are other men in the Bible that did this very thing where Elijah, Enoch, and Paul were taken to the Heavenly Kingdom in human form, but I believe transitioned to Spirit. These correlations remind me of Isaiah 55:9 where the Most High says, *"For as the heavens are higher than the earth, so are my ways higher than your ways, and my thoughts than your thoughts."* Sirius is the brightest star in our night sky and 8.611 light years higher than the Earth! The Most High set mankind apart from all Creation and imbued us with abilities the ancient's cultivated and modern-day Pharisees have hidden from the masses.

All we need to do now is reclaim our ancestor's ancient practices and follow the teachings of our great Teacher. We are blessed to have the King from the Royal Family lay down His life for us (as a demonstration) and He did it because He loved His Creation and this world. Psalm 139:14, *"I will praise thee; for I am fearfully, wonderfully made: marvelous are thy works; and that my soul knoweth right well."* Now we begin to see pictures like the one below in a whole new light.

When you saw the picture of the Egyptian in space what did you notice? Academia called this a "boat" the Egyptian is riding in death, but that is not correct. The ancients left us the ability to decipher these things when our civilization was ready and not before. Our

understanding of these ancient things is predicated on our own understanding of science and more specifically quantum physics.

Therefore, every twenty years our understanding of the Universe changes. What the ancient Egyptian is standing on in space is not a boat or a barge for this illustration. What sense would it make bringing a barge to space? That sounds as practical as a submarine with a screen door!

These are spiritual based images and used for a different type of matter. What the ancient Egyptian is traveling through is what quantum physicist call in Einstein-Rosen-Bridge or otherwise known as a wormhole. A wormhole is a concept that represents a solution of the Einstein field equations: a non-trivial structure linking separate points in space-time. A wormhole can be visualized as a tunnel with two ends, each at separate points in space-time (i.e. different locations and/or different points of time), or by a transcendental bi-jection of the space-time continuum.

Wormholes are consistent with the general theory of relativity, but whether wormholes exist remains to be seen, yet the ancient Egyptian barque is remarkably similar to the theories of Einstein. A wormhole could connect extremely long distances such as a billion light-years or more, short distances such as a few meters, different universes, or different points in time. The caveat is nothing physical can travel through the wormhole, but the spirit can! In my opinion, the Universal design calls for souls to travel in space. The Most High is sitting on his Throne giggling as humankind invests billions to travel through deep space physically.

I would not be surprised if Star Trek is a comedy in the Heavenly realm. Psalm 2:4, *"He who sits in the heavens laughs; the Lord holds them in derision."* This likewise demonstrates to us the ancient Egyptians were

Ancient Egyptian Symbol for the Einsetin Rosen Bridge Wormhole

into otherworldly development and we can conclude from their insight into the soul, they were very best in class. If we continue to accept the European perspective on the ancients, we will stay in spiritual darkness literally.

Please note the ancient Egyptians were spiritually traveling to the same part of space the Bible addresses. Job 38:31, "*Canst thou bind the sweet influences of Pleiades, or loose the bands of Orion?*" I would like to add special emphasis nothing in this presentation should negate or undermine the teachings of Jesus

Christ. He was and will always be the perfect example of spiritual training, and I have no doubt of His Divinity.

What I am submitting is Jesus also came to teach us how to activate our spiritual selves, hence being born again. This conversion to our spiritual bodies would inevitably and irrevocably end all reliance on *anything* material and activate our spiritual capabilities. If we look at the practices Christ taught His Disciples, it is the same formula we must follow. Matthew 17:20-21, "*20 And Jesus said unto them, Because of your unbelief: for verily I say unto you, If ye have faith as a grain of mustard seed, ye shall say unto this mountain, Remove hence to yonder place; and it shall remove; and nothing shall be impossible unto you. 21 Howbeit this kind goeth not out but by* **prayer and fasting**.

This means the Most High is aiding in the process via your prayers and the toughest part is the fasting. It took Jesus 40 days to break His dependency on food and sustained Himself on natural Earth water from most likely mineral rich lakes, streams, or underground springs. The human body of Jesus switched over to photosynthesis like a plant and began to convert sunlight into energy for His body. Jesus, cryptically referred to this very thing when the Disciples begged Him to eat food.

John 4:31-32, 31 Meanwhile his disciples urged him, "Rabbi, *eat something.*" 32 But he said to them, "*I have food to eat that you know nothing about.*" Therefore, I believe there has been tampering with Scripture through omission. Jesus loved the Disciples and was their Teacher. Why wouldn't He just tell them His body could now sustain itself on sunlight for energy?

Does that sound logical to you? The omissions are even more egregious when you reference a book not included in the Bible. The Nag Hammadi Library carries *The Book of Thomas the Contender*, and it quotes Jesus as saying, "*If you do not fast as regards the world, you will not find the kingdom. If you do not observe the Sabbath as a Sabbath, you will not see the father.*" Even in books not included from the Bible Jesus is stressing that *fasting* is key to be born again!

Jesus then adds another requirement when he states the word *water*. Jesus made it clear to be born again you must follow his instructions to the word. John 3:4-6, 4 Nicodemus said to him, "*How can a man be born when he is old? Can he enter a second time into his* mother's womb and be born?" 5 Jesus answered, "*Truly, truly, I say to you, **unless one is born of water and the Spirit**, he cannot enter the kingdom of God. 6 That which is born of the flesh is flesh, and that which is born of the Spirit is spirit.*"

Baptism is the beginning, and it also includes just sustaining yourself on sunlight and water. There are men walking the Earth who eat less food and only Sun gaze and drink vitamin/mineralized water. Science is learning melanated skin acts like solar panels (Orenstein, 2011) and has already gained a deeper understanding of human skin, sunlight, and Vitamin D production. Forty days has a sacred relevance in Judaism due to this period stated many times in: Genesis, Exodus, Leviticus, Deuteronomy, and Numbers, to the development of prophets.

This is the reason I am studying all ancients, even though I have exhibited the starting points of otherworldly development it does not supersede the lessons of Christ at any rate. In fact, what I am submitting are missing links to complete our spiritual transformation and sustaining healthy minds, bodies, and spirits. We have great power locked inside our genes, and our goal should be unlocking it. If an ancient man did it, then modern man can do it!

We should try to receive daily safe sunlight. There is a relationship between the endocrine system, dreams, and spiritual activation. The ancient Egyptians mastered spiritual activation of their bodies and could travel the cosmos. Spiritual activation includes conditioning the endocrine system with proper diet, exercise, and Sun gazing.

Finally, I believe a healthy endocrine system means a disease-free body. The ancients went out of their way to emphasize the pineal gland, tree of life and the Sun. These must be the mechanism of great change in the human body activating our DNA to our spiritual bodies.

Science of Melanin

"Melanin can absorb any type of energy, including mechanical, and also any wavelength." - Arturo Solis Herrera and Paola E Solis Arias

Melanin is classically defined as *a dark brown to black pigment occurring in the hair, skin, and iris of the eye in people and animals.* It is responsible for the tanning of skin exposed to sunlight. The scientific community progressively matured into a greater understanding of melanin, but even the most mature scientist will tell you there is so much more to learn. We are all born with varying degrees of melanin, but genetics have proven the most melanated race is the Black race.

The Sumerians referred to themselves as *ùg sag gíg-ga*, which means "the black-headed people." Herodotus states in a few passages that the Egyptians were a black/dark (Lloyd, 1750) Negroid people. According to most translations, Herodotus states that a Greek oracle was known to be from Egypt because she was "black," that the natives of the Nile region are "black with heat", and that Egyptians were "black-skinned with woolly hair." Based on ancient eyewitness testimony and research these civilizations possessed a high degree of melanin.

I mention Egypt because they were the forerunners of a synthesis of ancient practices that appear to be the foundation for the modern-day Christian religion. The irony is the keys to this knowledge are hidden in plain view and the true applications never promoted in public. This way these abilities would seem only attainable for Jesus, Disciples, and prophets of the Bible; however, Jesus said, John 14:12-14 (KJV), 12 *Verily, verily, I say unto you,* **He that believeth on me, the works that I do shall he do also; and greater works than these shall he do;** *because I go unto my Father. 13 And whatsoever ye shall ask in my name, that will I do, that the Father may be glorified in the Son. 14 If ye shall ask anything in my name, I will do it.*

Right there Jesus told us this is a process with rules that must be followed. Jesus also made it clear we would do more "miracles" than He performed because he was returning to His Kingdom. We must break our reliance on food to switch our spiritual self on which is very similar to ketogenesis or fasting. As a result, the body goes from the fed to the fasted state the liver switches from an organ of carbohydrate utilization and fatty acid synthesis to one of fatty acid oxidation and ketone body production. In essence, ketogenesis tricks the body into believing it is fasting.

Science shows the fasting human body changes over to melanin-based photosynthesis. Why does the human body switch over to mass melanin production? The regular reaction of the human body when nourishment vitality is disturbed is to naturally react by preparing the human body to retain light vitality. John 8:12, *"Then spake Jesus again unto them, saying, I am the light of the world: he that followeth me shall not walk in darkness, but **shall have the light of life.**"*

When you fast, it improves the function of insulin by raising adiponectin and (cAMP) cyclic adenosine monophosphate. This is a second messenger important in many biological processes and shown to improve melanin production in the skin even without stimulation from sunlight. There are cases where people begin to tan without any light source due to fasting! Jesus, fasting for forty days sounds extreme, but He broke His reliance on food source energy and turned His melanin on full power for light energy reception.

"The Healing of the Paralytic"
Dura Europas, Syria
c. 235 A.D.

I have coined the term, "spirit-genesis" to define the human body's energy consumption switchover to spirit/light moving forward. I would also like to revisit an earlier illustration when I showed the Assyrian Ashur in the Sun holding the bow and aiming an arrow. This arrow did not have an arrowhead, but a shape that remarkably matches the dove associated with the Holy Spirit. It should be clear the Holy Spirit dove is associated with the Sun.

Acts 2:2-4, 2 *And suddenly there came a sound from heaven as of* a rushing mighty (solar) wind, *and it filled all the house where they were sitting. 3 And there appeared unto them* **cloven tongues like as of fire**, *and it sat upon each of them. 4 And they were all filled with the Holy Ghost, and began to speak with other tongues, as the Spirit gave them utterance.*

The Sun is known to have both a *wind* and *fire,* so you must agree this lends credence to the Sun is where the Holy Spirit emanates from, in addition to the ancient match to the postmodern Holy Spirit dove. I believe these "doves" shooting in and out of the Sun have been video recorded. There was a YouTube producer out of Denver, Colorado, named *Magnet Flipper*. He used a Remington spotting scope and a technique he called, "Sunlight ablation" to record orbs of light streaking into and out of the Sun.

Magnet Flipper's video showed "white orbs" streaking in and out of the Sun. Is it possible once the melanin level is high enough in the human body and the heart is purified through fasting and prayer the solar doves become attracted to the human soul? This means no more food for energy and switching over to sunlight

Neo-Assyrian 9th or 8th century B.C. of the Sun shooting out the "dove" compared to the modern-day symbol for the Holy Spirit

and water. If you are interested in seeing the video of this solar phenomenon visit YouTube and type in: "Infrared UFO shot in daylight – Magnet Flipper."

The material system we live in is designed to keep us out of the Sun and our bodies in a state of solar malnutrition. Earlier in the book, I introduced the Queensland University study announcing that melanin is a super bioconductor of electricity and magnetism. "Melanin can talk' to both electronic and ionic control circuitry and hence can provide that connection role," said Professor Meredith about the study's finding, the culmination of ten years of research and experiments.

It appears the Most High has created a melanin-based photosynthetic molecular skin suit for humans. I believe this also proves that suntan lotion is harmful to the light absorption process. When the body has received enough light the skin's response is to send discomfort signals to the brain. Suntan lotion disrupts this process because it is such an extreme pigment change the human body was not accustomed.

Sun tan lotion is a false replacement for melanin and skin cancer has been on the rise ever since the advent of suntan lotions and sprays. Filmmaker Tom Leveritt used an ultraviolet camera to show people how suntan lotion looks on their skin. If you could see in the ultra-violet spectrum, when you go to the beach you would see people walking around in "Blackface."

Scientists are learning more and more about melanin every year and are even comparing it to having photosynthesis capabilities for the human body. Meaning these findings give credence to evidence sunlight can provide the human body with energy stores

UV Camera: Suntan lotion is Black face

and like Jesus said, "**I have food to eat that you know
nothing about.**" It always kills me when I read Jesus
said this, as if He was holding out on the Disciples, and
had a Snickers bar tucked away in his tunic! We know
Jesus was talking about another food and I believe it was
the sunlight he was absorbing into the melanin
receptors of the skin, eyes and His pineal gland.

The pineal gland (Macchi MM, 2004) secretes
melatonin (through the conversion of serotonin) which

activates the pituitary gland to release MSH (melanocyte stimulating hormone). It is in the melanocytes that melanin is produced. Now we know the pineal gland initiates balance in the endocrine system and this is predicated on receiving healthy levels of safe sunlight. Once the pineal gland receives sufficient sunlight, it releases the hormone melatonin and the pituitary gland produces a mature melanin-forming cell, typically in the skin, but also found in the middle layer of the eye (the uvea), the inner ear, meninges, bones, and heart.

Melanin is a key cell to maintain balanced health in the human body and it all begins with sunlight. In other words, find a way to observe the sunrise and the sunset because your endocrine system feeds off it and in turn creates melanated cells. This means there is a direct connection between the endocrine system and melanin's role in gene expression. Science states melanin's role in gene expression with the skin, but what about other organs?

Science understands melanin plays a role in the physical senses, but it also plays a role in the spiritual senses. Remember the "tree of life" in the human brain that sits next to the pineal gland? Is it possible that combination of low voltage coupled with ultra-violet radiation on melanated skin activates spiritual senses? The "tree of life" is the brain sensing organ and if transformed raises its signal to the spiritual realm.

What we can deduct from ancient Egyptian hieroglyphs is they wore shorted kilts and were barefoot when Sun gazing. This exposed melanated skin to the solar rays and they held a copper ankh in one hand while the copper was-scepter was inserted into the Earth. In addition to these tools, the ancient Egyptians sun gazed bathing the optic nerve and saturated the eyes and pineal gland with solar radiation, at sunrise and at sunset.

In Malachi 4:1-3, where it says, "*For, behold, the day cometh, that shall burn as an oven; and all the proud, yea, and all that do wickedly, shall be stubble: and the day that cometh shall burn them up, saith the Lord of hosts, that it shall leave them neither root nor branch. 2 But unto you that fear my name shall the Sun of righteousness arise with healing in his wings; and ye shall go forth and grow up as calves of the stall. 3 And ye shall tread down the wicked; for they shall be ashes under the soles of your feet in the day that I shall do this, saith the Lord of hosts.*"

This prophecy speaks of a solar event where the solar rays initiate a transmutation of DNA, which causes an instantaneous change to human form. Is it not interesting a solar event is a catalyst for human evolution? There is also a relationship between Biblical prophecy and another ancient prophecy. 1 Corinthians 15:52, states, "*52 In a moment, in the twinkling of an eye, at the last trump: for the trumpet shall sound, and the dead shall be raised incorruptible, and we shall be changed.*"

This prophecy involves *sound* as a trigger to a global event which changes all of mankind . . . in an instant! There is also evidence melanin converts sound into light and this lends credence to the plausibility melanin can change DNA. September 20, 1989, National Institutes of Health published, The DNA base sequence changes induced by mutagenesis with ultraviolet light have been determined in a gene on a chromosome of cultured Chinese hamster ovary (CHO) cells. (Romac, 1989)

Presenting the scientific evidence ultraviolet radiation can change how genes express themselves! Now we can gain scientific insight to Malachi 4:1-3 and 1 Corinthians 15:52 and realize these are events of extreme sunlight and sound. Greater clarification can be gleaned from Isaiah 30:26 where the state of the Sun is defined in great detail. Here it states, "*Moreover the light of the moon shall be as the light of the sun, and the **light of the sun shall*** *be sevenfold, as the light of seven days, in the day that the LORD bindeth up the breach of his people, and healeth the stroke of their wound."*

There is another reference to healing with the Sun as in Malachi 4:1-3 and this event must change how our existing genes are expressed or quite possibly activating DNA known as junk? It also begs the question of what kind of healing will take place? I submit it is a good practice to condition our bodies through sun-gazing prior to these two prophetic solar events. The ancients were clearly aware of DNA and the relationship to the Sun and the pineal gland as transformers of the human body.

Finally, melanin is an amazing molecule to have in the human body and we all have various amounts of it. Some people are darker than others which means they can (Sayer Ji, 2012) create energy quicker, but like the story of the rabbit versus the turtle, the moral is, slow and steady wins the race which fits in with the safe Sun gazing methodology. Meaning a disciplined daily approach will eventually unlock the Kingdom within, in conjunction with the prayer, fasting, and the proper tools (copper ankh and was scepter) used by the ancients.

If the earliest European archeologist investigations were not hindered by prejudice and a disdain for all melanated things would probably be more advanced in spirit. It was this very hatred for Black cultures which caused the door to be shut into deeper spiritual insights and customs. These ancient cultures were vilified and called Sun worshippers when there was an obvious method to the madness. Many scholars are coming to the conclusions Abraham's ancestors were rulers who came out of Africa and that they were devotees of a faith that finds fulfillment in Jesus Christ, the Son of God. (Linsley, 2012)

Where I diverge from many of these researchers and scholars is where it comes to the Sun. I believe there is a common thread between Christianity and not just ancient Egypt, but the Sumerian lore. Many of these other scholars see the Sun solely as an emblem, but an emblem for what? Their short-sighted view missed the Sun as a catalyst to spiritual transformation!

Finally, these are all dark-skinned civilizations that skin was immersed in sunlight wearing kilts and clothing which allowed skin to be exposed to the sunlight. This was by design and provided them with solar infusion. The Sun was more than just an emblem to these cultures, but a gift. The melanin coursing with electromagnetic energy and endocrine chemical release modulated how ancient DNA expressed itself. Most likely culminating into spiritual transformation.

Prayer

Jeremiah 33:3

Call to me and I will answer you and tell you great and unsearchable things you do not know.

Prayer is the most powerful weapon at the disposal of humankind. The Universe is constructed of mental energy controlled by the Creator. Science is slowly coming to this conclusion learning things like no matter how vast the space electrons can communicate with each other instantaneously. Lending credence to the belief the Most High hears our prayers the moment we release them.

If you have activated the Kingdom within you would have direct contact with the Power of the Throne. Remember Jesus said in Matthew 28:18, "*And Jesus came and spake unto them, saying, All power is given unto me in heaven and in earth.*" This means we have access to this Power through Jesus, yet no one has been able to demonstrate this Power in two thousand years! Jesus used prayers to heal, cast out demons, call upon angels, create spontaneous matter, change the quantum state of matter, fly, teleport, and raise the dead.

When it comes to spirit, for every *need* there is a prayer, which gets answered and at times Power is manifest through us or others. One of the most interesting cases of prayer in the Bible is Mark 9:29 where certain demons can only be removed with prayer and fasting. There is also a scientific fasting to brain connection here. Why did Jesus *need* to fast in order for a prayer to work?

Is it possible the human brain (HAGERTY, 2009) consistently needs fresh neurons to increase the bandwidth for some prayers? Is it what comes back through you that require the fresh neurons? Also, when fasting, the pineal gland secretes more melatonin which creates more melanin. Mark Mattson, the current Chief of the Laboratory of Neuroscience at the National Institute on Aging and a professor of Neuroscience at The Johns Hopkins University commented on this very thing.

"Fasting is a challenge to your brain, and your brain responds to that challenge by adapting stress response pathways that help your brain cope with stress and disease risk. The same changes that occur in the brain during fasting mimic the changes that occur with regular exercise — both increase the production of protein in the brain

(neurotrophic factors), which in turn promotes the growth of neurons, the connection between neurons, and the strength of synapses." - Mattson (Walia, 2015)

Jesus knew how to master the potential of the human body and He knew the secret of mastering all forms of prayer while incarnated in the human body. There are six-hundred and fifty prayers listed in the Bible and the Bible documents Jesus praying twenty-fives times during His ministry. Prayer is also a conversion tool to prepare our hearts and minds for entry into a Kingdom where righteousness is the law of the land.

Prayer and meditation during Sun gazing conditions our behavioral response to being righteous. The most common side effect of Sun gazing is a sense of peace and calmness. In fact, it is an overwhelming sense of tranquility which allows the prayers to flow through the heart. Imagine meditating on one proverb while Sun Gazing? You would peacefully connect with the Son while speaking to His Light.

I mentioned the Book of Proverbs because the Biblical proverbs have origin in ancient Egyptian proverbs. In fact, according to the "Cultural Backgrounds Study Bible" King Solomon recited proverbs spoken by the ancient Egyptians! Christianity was born on the banks of the Nile, but the ancient Egyptians spoke the same truths long before the birth of Christianity. It is my opinion since the Book of Proverbs borrows from ancient Egypt they were not always pagan.

The Book of Proverbs is a guideline for morals, values, and wisdom. In order to spiritually enter the Kingdom of the Most High you must be righteous. Prayer is the great conditioner for retraining your heart and mind. There is a field of study called "neurotheology" where professionals study the brains of people who pray and meditate.

Dr. Andrew Newberg is a neuroscientist at the University of Pennsylvania and author of the book *How God Changes Your Brain*. For over a decade he scanned the brains of religious people. Dr. Newberg's scientific approach included injecting a dye into a person praying in order to trace the blood flow into the brain. Dr. Newberg's subject was Scott McDermott, a United Methodist minister who he placed in a Single-photon emission computed tomography scanner. (M.D., 2010)

Dr. Newberg was not surprised with the results because he saw increased activity in the frontal lobe of the brain. What did fascinate Dr. Newberg was when a monk meditated in the scanner. The parietal lobes went

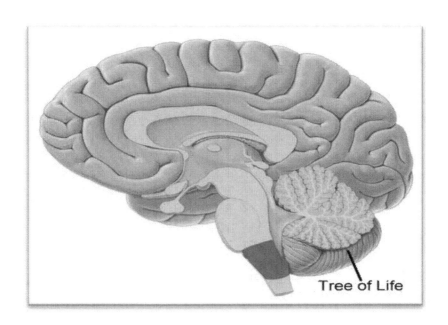

Tree of Life

dark which are responsible for the sensory information. Remember previously in the book I presented the "tree of life?"

Well, this area went dark suggesting the physical senses switched off to spiritual senses! Monks are adepts in prayer and meditation, so they can raise their signals to the highest level in the "tree of life." Is this scientific evidence the soul of the monk left their body? I am not sure about that, but I do believe it is evidence human consciousness can ascend the tree of life and sense of spirit.

Since the parietal lobes were dark in the scanner it means no senses processed in the brain, yet the spiritual experience was in motion. This also supports the notion prayer leaves the physical world and travels to the spiritual realm. How can physical surveillance monitor that of what happens in spirit? Prayer is the invisible act of requisition which in turn leads to receiving if the motives are righteous.

There is a Mayan prophecy, from Jaguar priest, regarding, December 21, 2012, that speaks of a change in consciousness and directly references raising the signal in the *tree of life* to the highest level resulting in a new consciousness. This is what the Mayan prophecy stated, *"When their signal is raised up high, when they raise it with the Tree of Life, all will suddenly change in one blow. And the successor of the first tree of the land will appear and the change will be manifested for all."* This is certainly a diversion from the classical understanding of the "tree of life" from a Kabbalah perspective, but one where scientific physiology and spiritual connotation meet in the middle.

Prayer and meditation are the conditioning mechanisms of raising the signal through the tree of life in the brain. This also brings a new perspective to Adam and Eve "eating" the apple from the tree of knowledge. As a result, they gained "new senses," and I believe exactly the purpose of the tree of life in the human brain. Prayer and meditation are like nurturing and stimulating the tree of life for spiritual sensing.

I liken this to starting out in the gym as a beginner and years later everything on your body is ripped. The by-product is righteousness in the moral fiber of the human heart. The "tree of life" is conditioned to upgrade the brain with functioning spiritual senses, while being righteous gains you entrance into the Heavenly Kingdom. Through this journey, I now understand the human construct in a new light . . . no pun intended. The ancients and classical artist revered Sirius as the homeworld of all souls. The Bible mentions Orion four times in Scripture, and the Pleiades star system is mentioned as well. Why was this particular location in space chosen to have such a storied relationship with the denizens of the Earth?

How do prayers reach a place in space 8.61 light years away? Is it plausible the energy from Sirius powers our Sun and the Holy Spirit (dove) is what comes out of the Sun? If we trust the ancient understanding, there is a relationship between Sirius and the Sun. I wonder if the Sun is the transport mechanism for prayers to the Orion spirit realm?

What we have not seen is prayer leading to healings like the ones mentioned in the Bible; where men born blind were prayed for and gained sight. There were also cases where people could not walk from birth but gained this ability through prayer. The problem we are having is not with prayer, but perhaps how and when to pray.

These are questions we should ask because it has been two thousand years since anybody has possessed the capacity to show what Jesus guaranteed humanity could demonstrate, yet the majority take after huckster ministers, prosperity preachers, and self-delegated "watchmen" who can exhibit only cash accumulation. While my wife was dying from inflammatory breast cancer, many people prayed for her recovery. One of the most diligent prayer warriors was her mother who would wake up daily at 5:00 AM to pray. I was shocked to walk by her room when she stayed with us, and she was on her knees, praying in Spanish.

Even her prayers proved to be ineffective, and three other churches prayed incessantly for a miracle. They were all highly committed to her recovery, and I do not doubt the sincerity of any of them, yet none of them could replicate the healings of Jesus or His Disciples. I concluded after her death there is a missing link and it needs to be identified. Jesus, John the Baptist, and Moses would all spend time in the Sun praying and meditating.

When John the Baptist baptized Jesus in Matthew 3:16 the Heavens opened, and it was stated, *"he saw the Spirit of God descending like a dove, and lighting upon him."* Previously, in the book, I submitted illustrations of the dove-like arrow the Assyrian Sun god used to represent what shoots out of the Sun. Before John the Baptist baptized Jesus, he prayed to the Most High under the Sun. The Vatican had a reason to remove the Sun element from spiritual cultivation.

The Light, which is the Sun, is the second thing the Most High produced to create life in the physical world. All things have duality in His Creation, and so does the Sun. If it has physical properties, then it has spiritual properties as well. Which I believe includes transforming the DNA of humanity to that of Spirit.

We should pray to the Most High while Sungazing and bring our needs to Him in this manner. We have plenty of examples of men who did this in the Bible, yet we do not follow them and wonder why miracle prayers are ineffective. If we closely follow the life of Christ, we know He would speak miracles into existence, and he demonstrated these seven times in the Bible. Jesus promised humanity has the same abilities if we follow

His ways and prayer/meditation under the Sun is one of them.

Prayer was a weapon against invisible forces, and some were natural, while others were unnatural. We as a people must be in the right state for our prayers to be effective. Prayer conditions the human heart in conformance with the Divine Mind and must regularly be practiced to take hold. Once this happens you become a candidate for that Holy exchange with the Sun.

At this point is when the "dove" shoots out and transforms you forever. Imagine how powerful your prayers will be then! There are many prayers to learn, and we should focus on learning them. I look at them as a metaphysical library where we should know which ones to recite. Just like a seasoned black belt knows what move to make when threatened.

Sound of the Sun

Do you know that our soul is composed of harmony?

Leonardo da Vinci,
Notebooks (1451-1519)

The moment of Creation used two forces, and the first was sound (frequency), and the other was light (radiation). I believe this same formula applies to our spiritual transformation. Cymatics is the investigation of obvious sound vibration and demonstrates the transformational idea of sound and matter. Cymatics is a merging science with an (Arnold, 2014) ancient footprint.

I am reminded of Ecclesiastes 1:9 (NIV), 9 What has been will be again, what has been done will be done again; there is nothing new under the sun. The ancients used sound to move giant stones like the one in the Pyramid of Giza. Edward Leedskalnin claimed he knew the secrets of the ancient Egyptians. He was a Latvian immigrant to the United States, self-taught engineer, and sculptor who single-handedly built the Coral Castle

in Florida, added to the National Register of Historic Places in 1984.

Leedskalnin was a petite man who moved limestone rock that weighed over two tons by himself! It is theorized the ancients negated the electrons of an object using sound, electricity, and magnetism. Leedskalnin kept his secrets until his death and only worked at night to avoid observation. However, one-night curious children attempted to watch him, but only heard him "whistling" while he worked. (Emery., 2015)

I was fascinated by how the ancient moved stones that weighed tons and precisely stack them where you

Coral Castle (formerly known as Rock Gate)

cannot even slide a piece of paper between them! The ancients did not just use sound for construction, but for spiritual transformation. Light and sound are the mechanisms to activate our dormant spiritual DNA. The Essenes combined chanting with Sun gazing to activate the pineal gland.

"Barefoot healing practices of the Essenes happened at lakes, ponds, waterfalls, rivers or dry riverbeds for enhanced bioposure through direct, prolonged contact with the exposed piezoelectric stone. This practice is now scientifically recognizable as a biophotonic healing technique that makes use of low-level electrical ground currents for enhancing resonant nuclear reaction cascades responsible for the subtle luminosity of every living cell." (Putney, 2014)

Again, we are introduced to a barefoot connection with the Earth to facilitate a physical and spiritual change. Grasping the copper was-scepter as it is inserted into the ground, while Sun gazing and singing a hymn creates dual forces in the human body. The Russian biophysicist and atomic researcher Pjotr Garjajev and his partners likewise investigated the vibrational conduct of the DNA. Garjajev, experiment with the salamander and the frog went viral.

Garjajev in a controlled laboratory setting used a cold irradiated laser and beamed it through a salamander egg into a frog egg. To his surprise the frog egg matured and grew into a healthy adult salamander. This experiment proved the holographic nature of DNA. It also proved light and frequency can change DNA from one state to another. (Staff, 2011)

On a macro level the Sun and planetary vibration will play a role in the spiritual transformation of humans. This reminds me of 1 Corinthians 15:52, where it is said, *"In a moment, in the twinkling of an eye, at the* last trump: *for the trumpet shall sound, and the dead shall be raised incorruptible, and we shall be changed.*" I trust the actors at this moment will be the Sun and the Earth. Many people debate if zombies will be pouring out of cemeteries, but I submit that is not the case because many people are spiritually dead.

In my opinion, this means the dead's signal will be raised to the highest level in their "tree of life." If we follow Garjajev's model Sirius can beam a new genetic code through the Sun and mother Earth will emit a frequency. Even people that do not put in the work will have the opportunity to spiritually transform. It's only fair since we were born into a world where the keys to knowledge were hidden!

Mary Magdalene was an astute student of the teachings of Jesus and many Renaissance painters depict her with halo or Sun above her head. In my opinion Mary Magdalene was never given due credit for her role with Jesus or spiritual transformation, and the reason beings was that she was a woman. It is common to believe she was an adulterer or a whore, or even the mother of children with Jesus. People who believe this fail to recognize the moment the solar dove enters your body your DNA is activated to Spirit.

You are no longer driven by carnal desires because you are no longer operating from the flesh. In fact, you are operating closer to light. So, these common misperceptions are nothing more than people humanizing spiritual things they do not understand. Mary Magdalene is said to have been an advanced student of Jesus and was celebrated in Renaissance art as such. If she practiced what the Essenes practiced, then she too used light and sound to actuate her spiritual body.

Remember earlier in the book where Pope Innocent III dispatched crusaders to murder Christians in Carth, Southern France because they also practiced Sun gazing? You must also wonder how these teachings were introduced to this land. Jesus laid down His life for the sins of the world in Jerusalem. Yet, in the 12th century A.D., Pope Innocent III is eradicating Jesus and Essene, teachings from Jerusalem by mass murder.

Of course, there is a story explaining how teachings of Jesus made it to the shores of Southern France. It includes Mary Magdalene and it is not just supported by oral history but captured in paintings. I think this is major evidence because it explains how ancient knowledge of spiritual transformation was bridged to another continent. It also lends credence the Christians of Southern France Sun gazed because according to ancient documentation Jesus, the Essenes, and Mary Magdalene Sun gazed for spiritual transformation. The following is a story about *three* Mary's who arrived in Southern France:

After the death of Jesus, the disciples were spread to the four winds. Across the sea in Southern France, a myth arose. Legend says that a boat with no sails and no oars landed on the shores of Provence. Three women named Mary, including mother Mary and the Magdalene, along with Martha, Lazarus, and an Egyptian servant named Sarah are said to have landed at Saintes Maries-de-la-Mer, now named for the arrival of the "holy Mary's from the sea." The story goes that each settled in a different area of France, that Mary Magdalene herself started a church and retired to live out her days in a grotto on the high hill of Saint Baume. Why are so many modern seekers fascinated by this tale and by Mary Magdalene herself? (Lavino, 2007)

I think this is a major connection to how the teachings of Jesus embeds into the Southern France communities, (Purdon, 2016) including Sun gazing. The people of Southern France had arguably one of the most advanced Disciples in Mary Magdalene, and she demonstrated the power of the Spirit. We should be able to build a model of, anywhere the Disciples taught influenced a region, the teachings were subsequently squelched out by mass murder.

I would be remiss if I did not mention *The Gospel of Mary* and it is found in the *Berlin Gnostic Codex* (*Papyrus Berolinensis 8502*). This very important and well-preserved codex was discovered in the late-nineteenth century somewhere near Akhmim in upper Egypt. It was purchased in Cairo in 1896 by a German scholar, Dr. Carl Reinhardt, and then taken to Berlin (Owens, 1998). Many pages of this manuscript are missing, and I can only assume more "keys of knowledge" were lost, which would inevitably lead to spiritual transformation.

There is a connection between meditation and chanting with the Essenes and sound also followed Mary Magdalene in her spiritual transformation journey.

Jean-Yves Leloup is a theologian and founder of the Institute of Other Civilization Studies and the International College of Therapists. His books include "Jesus and Judas, The Sacred Embrace of Jesus and Mary", "The Gospel of Mary Magdalene", "The Gospel of Philip", and "The Gospel of Thomas." He lives in France, and he stated,

> *"Each morning a group of angels lifted Magdalene above the summit of the cliffs, where she could listen to the entire choir of angelic host, the divine sounds of original and continuing creation."* (Leloup, 2002)

There is a clear relationship between sound and spiritual cultivation and even the angels play a role in this. Over the years my investigative journey has introduced me to other energy-related phenomena. Such as, the higher you climb a mountain, the stronger the natural electrical field becomes. Some Biblical scholars claim the Ark of the Covenant was set high up in the mountains to recharge.

Even the Sun has its frequency, and you can easily hear it on YouTube. Space is a vacuum and has no sound. The radio waves emanating from the Sun are recorded and then converted to sound waves. The sound of the Sun sounds very similar to the "Om" sound on a loop! I believe Jesus taught His Disciples to climb high into mountains to meditate and receive the *sound* and *energy* from the Sun.

Modern science is now investigating how a range of electrical frequencies heal chronic wounds. This discovery reminds me of Star Trek and how the medical team would wave a device emitting a high frequency over an injury and it would instantly heal the injury. What modern scientist are learning is difficult to-recuperate wounds, like diabetic ulcers, putrefy due to deficient blood supply at the injury site. These wounds benefit from the electrical stimulus and promote the growth of blood vessels. (Cincinnati, 2014)

In the case of electrical current, the frequency is the number of times a sine wave repeats or completes, a positive-to-negative cycle. As you can see frequency (sound) is a powerful creative force of the Most High which can affect the human body down to the cellular level. Even when introduced to cymatics you learn that sound waves have a distinct geometric shape.

Johann Wolfgang von Goethe, (born August 28, 1749, Frankfurt am Main [Germany]—died March 22,

1832, Weimar, Saxe-Weimar), German poet, playwright, novelist, scientist, statesman, theatre director, critic, and amateur artist, considered the greatest German literary figure of the modern era. Goethe made a profound observation of music (sound) when he said, *"Music is liquid architecture; Architecture is frozen music."*

The emerging scientific investigation of cymatics is quite fascinating. Here you will witness the geometric shaped counterparts of soundwaves. Each tone has its own geometry and the higher the octave the more complex the design. In my opinion, this relates to spiritual transformation as well because the higher your consciousness becomes the more complex you become. Leaving behind the old geometry of the lower frequencies.

This means the music we listen to influences our human minds and bodies. It is debated if Plato made the following quote but if he did it certainly makes sense, in lieu of what we know about frequency and the human body. Plato, said, *"If you want to measure the spiritual depth of society, make sure to mark its music."* If Plato heard our music what would he say about our spiritual depth?

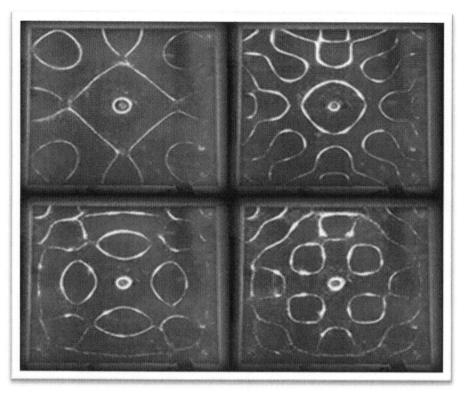

Natural geometric shapes of four tones

Frequencies also affect the shape of water molecules in our human body. There are studies where a bowl of water is bombarded with sound from a tone generator and geometric shapes take form in the water. Here are metrics for water in the human body. *Up to 60% of the human adult body is water. According to H.H. Mitchell, Journal of Biological Chemistry 158, the brain and heart are composed of 73% water, and the lungs are about 83% water. The skin contains 64% water, muscles* and *kidneys are 79%, and even the bones are watery: 31%.* (Perlman, 2016)

I trust Sun gazing for a prolonged period tunes the human physiology to that of the Sun. All though you cannot hear the Sun it is beaming frequency inside the human body along with the ultraviolet light. The water in the human body is transforming to the frequency of the Sun. This must somehow play a role in the pineal gland as well.

The Sun's frequency is 126.22 hz and its natural frozen in time shape is captured through symbols in ancient times. Proving the ancients were aware of it and the Pharisees and Vatican have hidden the meaning. When you see the shape of the Sun's frequency and the ancient constructs of it, you will agree they are remarkably similar. There is no denying this once you see it.

I laugh when I see this image of the water structure (Life, Water, The Sun, Frequency, and Flower of Life., 2016) of the Sun's frequency, because I say to myself, "Who is Sun worshipping now?" The Sun is nested and hidden inside Christianity where it has great importance and the powerless people traipse across

Photo of water structure exposed to the Sun's frequency of 126.22 hertz compared to a sarcophagus at the Catacombs of Domitilla circa 4th century A.D.

church pews as if they are on their way to spiritual transformation. If you do not realize the path to spiritual transformation is hidden, I have some sweet swamp land to sell you in Florida!

Psalm 2:4 NIV, *"The One enthroned in heaven laughs; the Lord scoffs at them."* We are truly a lost people, and it is time we reclaim our place in the Sun. Sound also plays a vital role in our spiritual cultivation on the road to our spiritual transformation. Thoughts and prayers can change the water structures in our bodies, and we can harmonically resonate with the

Sun's frequency. It should be apparent even the ancients knew this.

The Sun is the mechanism for humans to flower into our spiritual bodies. Once this happens, we will no longer be slaves to carnal desire, and we will turn back to being Sons of the Light. We are at a moment of our collective awakening, and we need only to return to the Sun.

Breathing

The nose is for breathing; the mouth is for eating.
~Proverb

Breathing is one of the most taken for granted autonomic functions of the human experience. It is so natural and life-sustaining it is only when threatened is it truly appreciated. When we are born, we are given our first breath, and when we die, we take our last breath. Unbeknown to most breathing is much more capabilities than just keeping the human body alive.

Breathing regulation can control stress, heart rate, and even brain waves. There is an association between breath controls the pineal organ and pituitary organ initiation. As of late, science found breath directly affects the development of Cerebrospinal (CSF) liquid. This liquid is an unmistakable, drab body liquid found in the cerebrum and spinal rope. It is created in the choroid plexuses of the ventricles of the brain and assimilated in the arachnoid granulations. (Robert Labensart, 2016)

The National Institutes of Health (Department of Anatomy, 1989) conducted a study, "Cerebrospinal fluid-contacting area of the deep pineal: effects of photoperiod." This study indicated an interaction between the cerebrospinal fluid (CSF) and associated ventricular structures and the deep pineal gland. This study more than suggests breathing is a critical component of pineal gland activation. The question now is what type of breathing is necessary when is Sun gazing? The answer to that is long slow deep breathing.

There are studies on deep breathing that have revealed long; slow, deep, breathing raises the alpha brain waves. Do you remember in the earlier chapter regarding the solar influence on the endocrine system? To reiterate the pineal gland chain reaction to the Sun causes serotonin production and then mixes to yield melatonin. When the human brain reaches an alpha wave state, it causes the production of melatonin.

Sungazing while long-deep-breathing adds a surplus of melatonin to the human body, in addition to the solar radiation bathing the optic nerve and stimulating the endocrine system. This breathing technique creates the optimal environment for the endocrine system to operate at peak capacity. Long-deep-breathing features in much Asian art

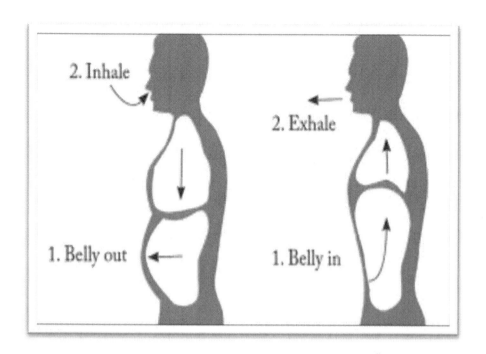

forms like martial arts and meditation. It is through control and mastering of breath many amazing human feats are possible.

Meditating on a prayer verse while breathing and Sungazing is the best practice. After a certain point of long-deep-breathing, your brain will transition to alpha waves, and the prayer will become engrained in your subconscious. Alpha brainwaves are the ideal brain state for learning and reduce depression and boost creative thinking. Combining prayer, breathing, and sun gazing into a continuous event moment will certainly have positive effects on the human body.

The human body is elevated by deep breathing should we not expect Scriptural characters practiced this too? Beginning with the book of Genesis in the Old Testament (Genesis 24:63) it is stated that Isaac goes out to meditate: *"And Isaac went out to meditate in the fields at the eventide, and he lifted up his eyes, and saw, and behold the camels were coming."* Also, in Joshua 1:8, it is stated: *"This book of the law shall not depart out of thy mouth; but thou shalt meditate therein day and night, that thou mayest observe to do according to all that is written therein; for then thou shalt make thy way prosperous, and then thou shalt have good success."* Throughout the Psalms, there are at least 14 verses, which talk about meditation. (Meditation and the Old Testament, 2013)

Many Christians balk at meditation and consider it pagan, but as you can see this is not the case. Deep breathing and meditation go hand-in-hand with your spiritual cultivation. While deep breathing transitions brain waves into the alpha state it is the meditation which entrains the human thought process on spiritual things. Jesus positively would have been acquainted with meditation while he was growing up, in lieu of the fact it is also stated in the Torah.

As a Jewish Rabbi, he would have completely comprehended the activities of Isaac meditating in the fields. There were various individuals in Jerusalem amid Jesus' life that He would have met with, and who might have comprehended the advantages of meditation. Many scholars trust Jesus made a trip to India amid his life and learned at various Buddhist Temples because a considerable lot of His teachings He told after his arrival was like the lessons of the Buddha. The Buddha, or "enlightened one," was born Siddhartha (which means "he who achieves his aim") Gautama to a large clan called the Shakyas in Lumbini, (today, modern Nepal) in the 6th century B.C.

Jesus was giving the Sermon on the Mount. He *meditated* and demonstrated this to His Disciples. I believe Jesus went high into the desert for solitude, Sun, and meditation for forty days. While in the desert Jesus prayed for forty days and nights and I assume this included meditating while Sungazing. Matthew 6:5, trained the Disciples to pray in secret and use few words.

As you can see breathing, prayer, and meditation are part of the system to elevate the human mind. *As goes the mind, as goes the soul.* Breathing deeply will need to be practiced because most people do not breath the proper way. Sungazing, prayer, meditation should all happen at the same moment with the objective of actuation of our spiritual selves.

Ankh and Was-Scepter

"God has made us to be conduits of his grace. The danger is in thinking the conduit should be lined with gold. It shouldn't. Copper will do."

John Piper, Desiring God: Meditations of a Christian Hedonist

This chapter will be the most controversial chapter in this book because it is not proven. I will be relying on the ancient accounts and scientific findings for evidence. The ancient Egyptians left voluminous illustrations of humans and gods holding apparatus. Many European academics claimed the ankh was nothing more than a symbol for the key of life.

Present day prehistorian now accepts the ankh and was-scepter made from copper. Copper is a soft, malleable, and ductile metal with very high thermal and electrical conductivity. This tool complements the melanated skin, which is a superconductor of electromagnetic energy. I believe the loop in the ankh allowed the electromagnetic energy to oscillate as it coursed through the human melanated skin. This brings credence to the belief the ankh was more than just a symbol for life.

We can all agree with walking on the beach barefoot in the Sun elicits a calming effect on the soul. As previously stated in this book the solar rays set off a chain reaction in the endocrine system resulting in the production of hormones that relax and promotes peacefulness in the human endocrine system. The ancients took this to another level and perfected the science of Sun gazing in conjunction with tools. I believe facilitated a genetic transformation in the human body.

I presented ancient artifacts with a common theme of the: Sun, pineal gland, and DNA. These artifacts spanned from the earliest known civilizations leading up to the ancient Egyptians. They have provided a wellspring of solar teachings leading to a spiritual journey to the Sirius constellation, where the Heavenly Kingdom can be found. These elements are where I will be the string tying together already picked ancient flowers for modern spiritual transformation.

I cannot do any worse to our current spiritual condition where the ancient spiritual demonstration is nonexistent. It reminds me of saying from a retired Admiral who was full of sayings, *"It's like giving a dead man an enema, it can't hurt."* The ancients were closer to the beginning of civilization than us, which makes them closer to the truth. The early cultures passed down the necessary teachings so post cultures would operate at a spiritually high level.

Ancient artwork embodied DNA change through the pineal gland by the Sun. The earliest representations of the Sun showed Shamash holding a ring which looked like the precursor to the ankh of ancient Egypt and the Coptic cross of Christianity. Ashur, the Assyrian representation of the Sun was also holding a ring. There must be a purpose of the ring in hand about the Sun the ancients were well aware.

What happens when holding this ring while sun-gazing? The ancient Egyptians took this a step further and held a was-scepter or staff in their other hand. When analyzing the end of the was-scepter or staff, it resembles an electrical prong where the end must be inserted into the Earth. I heard a rumor, and I have not been able to substantiate it when Napoleon was on his scientific expedition to the Pyramids of Giza, he recovered a functional ankh enclosed in a solid gold case.

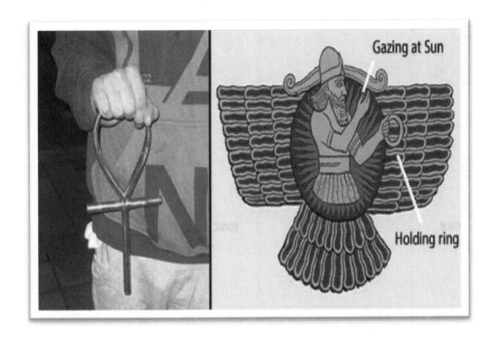

This makes sense because copper is conductive, and this ankh configures with a *djed,* the Egyptian word for pillar, but I think battery. The Baghdad battery is like the djed and it was less than 1 volt. Military scientists are using electrical brain stimulators (Sample, 2016) to enhance the mental skills of their staff. The objective is to boost the performance of aircrews, drone operators, and others in demanding roles.

A weak current is pulsed through five electrodes to a brain stimulation kit into specific parts of the cortex. Weak current improves how neurons fire and improve cognitive ability. This account lends credence that ankhs with the djed could safely pulse weak current through highly melanated human skin. The shape of the ankh creates an oscillation loop for the person holding it.

The was-scepter is also made of copper and inserting it in the Earth would pull a subtle current from the Earth; this is called grounding. There are illustrations of the ancient Egyptians showing them barefoot for a skin connection to the Earth. Finally, the ancient Egyptians exposed as much skin as possible to the Sun and were illustrated wearing kilts. Melanin is superconductive, and the skin is the largest organ of the human body.

The melanin in the skin (C. H. Culp, 2008) will conduct the electromagnetic current around the human body. Even people who are melanin deficient could wear a linen hood top with linen pants, and the current would envelop the human body because the linen fabric (Hergenrather, 2010) is conductive. The first thing you need to do before you pursue the sun-gazing path is to visit your doctor. Make sure you have no obvious medical issues.

You should Sun gaze during safe hours, and this means respecting the safe hours (sunrise and sunset) at all times. You reduce eye damage risk when you Sun gaze at sunrise and up to an hour after. You can also Sun gaze at sunset and an hour before sunset. Sungaze at any other time and you will be putting your eyes at risk; because the UVB index is so high.

I would visit the eye doctor before starting so you will have a baseline for your eye history. The Bible states in Ecclesiastes 7:11, *"Wisdom, like an inheritance, is a good thing and benefits those who see the sun."* I think it is important to see the Sun regularly to increase wisdom and there is great mystery nested in this verse. What we know from a Biblical standpoint fasting is an excellent way to create new melanin cells in your body and skin. I look at this like a required bio-maintenance plan, which is required before and while Sun gazing to maximize benefits.

Fasting also creates new neural connections in the brain (Wilson, 2017) and resets the immune system (Wu, 2014) with fresh stem cells. If you plan to fast for 40 days, please review your plan with your doctor first! Safety should always come first, and this means checking with medical professionals first! People have died from not discussing their 40 days fast with a medical professional.

The 40 days fast is designed to break your body's dependency on solid food and does not mean to deprive your body of necessary proteins, amino acids, vitamins, and minerals. You can have all of these in a liquid form without breaking the rules. Most importantly, it should ward off you are harming yourself in any way. The human body requires protein to keep the muscles strong and to operate optimally, and that includes the heart muscle.

There are liquid proteins on the market like "Proteinex 15 Liquid Protein." Two tablespoons a day are sufficient to meet the daily protein consumption guidelines. There is also a liquid product, "Liquid Health Complete Multiple Natural Berry," which has the full spectrum of vitamins and folic acid necessary for healthy organs. Minerals are important for building strong bones, teeth, blood, skin, hair, nerve function, muscle and for metabolic processes. There is a liquid product called "ALPHA Mineral Health Support" which has 60 essential minerals.

I believe products like these should be taken during the 40 days fast and will maintain healthy body results with minimal energy decreases. Most of these come in a one-month supply, and you would need to purchase two of each. I think it is wonderful we are living in a time product like these can be purchased in a liquid form to reduce fasting risk. Normally the hunger for food pains ends after three or four days into the fast.

When my wife was dying, I did not eat for five days from the grief, and the hunger subsided on day three. It is very important to fast while Sungazing and we must follow the example Jesus demonstrated and following what I have suggested means doing it safely. Again, please share these products with your doctor and make sure a medical professional authorizes them for you.

There is also a correlation to Sun gazing and being born again. It takes nine months to follow the Sun gazing protocol consisting of ten second daily increments until reaching 45 minutes. After you reach nine months, you are complete and born again. This time you have filled your body with light and some people experience a reduced appetite for solid food.

In my opinion, Sun gazing does not replace solid eating, but to activate our spiritual selves. Even after transforming into Spirit, Jesus ate a piece of fish.

Certainly, not a bucket of chicken with a biscuit, but a very light treat for His stomach! Sun gazing with the ankh and was-scepter must activate dormant DNA in humans. Jesus was able to oscillate between the physical and the spiritual before and after his death.

When He returned to His Disciples after His crucifixion, He must have shifted to physical form where he experienced hunger! Let us look at Luke 24:35-48 (KJV), *35 And they told what things were done in the way, and how he was known of them in breaking of bread. 36 And as they thus spake, Jesus himself stood in the midst of them, and saith unto them, Peace be unto you. 37 But they were terrified and affrighted, and supposed that they had seen a spirit. 38 And he said unto them, Why are ye troubled? and why do thoughts arise in your hearts? 39 Behold my hands and my feet, that it is I myself: handle me, and see; for a spirit hath not flesh and bones, as ye see me have. 40 And when he had thus spoken, he shewed them his hands and his feet. 41* **And while they yet believed not for joy, and wondered, he said unto them, Have ye here any meat?** *42 And they gave him a piece of a broiled fish, and of a honeycomb. 43* **And he took it and did eat before them.**

Post-crucifixion Jesus went somewhere inside the Earth for three days. Some scholars agree this is a physical location, while others claim it is a spiritual location. I trust this was another dimensional area where the Spirit assemblage of Jesus entered; when Jesus returned to the flesh, His body-craved sustenance. Conversely, the human transforms into solar consumption when in a strictly spiritual state.

We must be able to survive much longer without food than our current science understands once in a solar consumption state. Jesus gave us a formula for being born again, and that is: baptism, fasting, prayer, meditating, and Sun gazing. The ancient Egyptians incorporated three energies into the process with the first being ultra-violet light, the second being earth current, and the third the human bodies electromagnetic field. Science now understands the ultra-violet light optimizes the endocrine system and the relationship to how genes express themselves.

If your goal is to Sungaze to feel better than you will. I was suffering from depression after the death of my wife and betrayal of people I thought close to me. The betrayal driven by my wife's family greed, an unethical attorney, and the minds of prejudice in the community. I was devastated watching this beautiful soul who gave me three beautiful sons succumb to the horrors of cancer.

During my grief rumors were spread by wife's unscrupulous family members and I became ostracized by some in the community. When the greedy plot was thwarted by the Most High, anonymous *Child Protective Services* calls began, and even my son's elementary school got in on it! All *Child Protective Service* allegations were proven to be unfounded. The only success the greedy family members had, was stealing my mail and stealing from my children's trust fund.

I am sharing these details so that you will understand my level of depression. I escaped from that toxic family, "frenemies," and a fickle community by leaving New York and relocating down south. I finally could begin to heal my deep wounds in peace. I remember feeling great depression every day until one day I Sungazed.

There is a park with a lake near my home, and I went there at sunset. I kid you not; I Sun gazed for ten seconds that evening and immediately could feel the difference! I became overcome with a sense of peace,

The park where I Sun gaze. He leadeth me to still waters.

and I slept deep that night. I was sold and decided to return the next evening.

Again, I experienced a great calming feeling, and I realized the depression was leaving me. I did everything by the Sun gazing book when I did it the first time. I went at sunset, and I was barefoot on the dirt. The third day it hit me that this whole scene reminded me of Psalm 23 (KJV) 23, *"The Lord is my shepherd; I shall not want. 2 He maketh me to lie down in green pastures: he leadeth me beside the still waters. 3 He restoreth my soul: he leadeth me in the paths of righteousness for his name's sake."*

I was lying on the green grass before I Sun gazed right next to a calm lake. After I finished Sungazing I felt like my soul was being restored because the depression was leaving me! It was a remarkable emotional feeling because I was accustomed to feeling depressed. If you are looking to regain a sense of calm and tranquility then Sun gazing is the way to go, however, the ancients have shown us there is much more to this, and it leads to the Kingdom within!

There is another world for us to communicate with and receive great power. Now we can understand how the Pyramids of Giza constructed without the intervention of "aliens." We should not be shocked by this notion because plans were sent from the Heavenly Kingdom in Orion to build the Holy Tabernacle and Noah's ark. It seems some academics are hell-bent on a theory of a physical alien presence on Earth, while they omit spiritual evidence from the ancients.

The late comedian/activist Dick Gregory said, "*If you ever want to find out what is happening in the news, watch it while it is happening because later on, the story will change.*" The ancients were closer to the beginning of humanity than we are, and we should meticulously study their beliefs, understandings, and applications.

The ancients lived in a time where they could talk to their ancestors. How was this possible?

I submit the ancients were able to travel in spirit to the Heavenly Kingdom in Orion. The ancient world is replete with unparalleled architecture that modern technology lacks the intellect to recreate. The ankh and the was-scepter were tools to connect to the Earth and the Heavens through man. In the below bas-relief you see the ankh, battery, and was-scepter.

All three of these tools must be necessary to transform the human body into a state where the human can oscillate between physical and spiritual states. This means a transition from a physical state to a spiritual state. In ancient Egypt, there were two distinctly separate schools for spiritual cultivation. One was for the royal families and priest while the other was for the common people.

This controlled knowledge and who had access to the process of communicating with the Kingdom. We must now begin to test this ancient practice *with* and *without* the weak current flowing through the ankh. We must keep in mind the earliest artifacts just show a man holding a ring and I am assuming it is made of copper.

The subsequent iterations had a bar added underneath the ring to the ankh we are familiar with today.

The ancients knew this information was priceless and preserved this knowledge in stone. Let us now go over the exact methodology for Sun gazing with the ankh and was-scepter. It is vital to follow the steps in sequence as taught by our great Teacher including narratives of His practices outside of the Bible. This will ensure us a successful tool utilization as proven in ancient times.

The modern church system has promoted this Truth which, is to get your heart right with the Most High. I generally accepted if there was just a single book a man should read in the Bible, that ought to be Proverbs. This book is a school of thought of how to live your life and treat people using Divine wisdom. If you lived the teachings in the Book of Proverbs you would live a righteous life.

Imagine my shock when I learned the Book of Proverbs shared many proverbs *from* the ancient Egyptians! We as humans must be righteous in order to enter the Heavenly Kingdom and the ancient Egyptians knew this. You will see many paintings of Jesus pointing at His heart and then upward, which I believe is at the

Sun. I believe the Most High controls the Earth *through* the Sun from Orion!

The energy that the Earth receives from the Sun is the basic cause of our changing weather. Solar heat warms the huge air masses that comprise large and small weather systems. The day-night and summer-winter cycles in the weather have obvious causes and effects (Biello, 2009). The Creator can control every weather outcome from the Sun, including earthquakes!

Job 37:9-16 *9 The stormy wind comes from its chamber, and the driving winds bring the cold. 10 God's breath sends the ice, freezing wide expanses of water. 11 He loads the clouds with moisture, and they flash with his lightning. 12 The clouds churn about at his direction. They do whatever he commands throughout the earth. 13* **He makes these things happen either to punish people or to show his unfailing love.** *14 "Pay attention to this, Job. Stop and consider the wonderful miracles of God! 15 Do you know how God controls the storm and causes the lightning to flash from his clouds? 16 Do you understand how he moves the clouds with wonderful perfection and skill?*

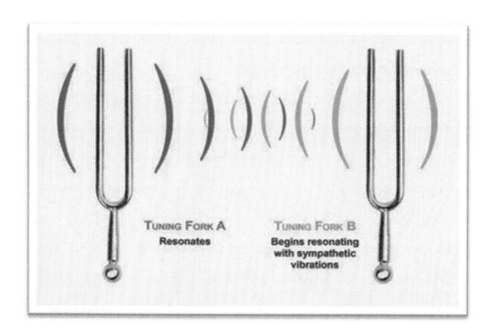

TUNING FORK A
Resonates

TUNING FORK B
Begins resonating
with sympathetic
vibrations

I believe even the waters were sent to the Earth from Orion and there is a water connection through sympathetic harmonics. Sympathetic resonance or sympathetic vibration is a harmonic phenomenon wherein a formerly passive string or vibratory body

responds to external vibrations to which it has a harmonic likeness. The best example is two pianos in a concert hall and on one of the pianos to bang on C# is the C# reverberates through the hall suddenly the C# on the other piano would begin to vibrate. I believe there is a connection there and I believe quantum physicist will learn quantum energy behaves like this no matter how vast the distance in space.

I say this to set up the understanding baptism is a connection to the Heavenly Kingdom through the water. It is like tagging an animal in the wild with a tracking device except the tag is the spirit of the water. John 3:5, "*Jesus answered, Verily, verily, I say unto thee, except a man be* **born of water and of the Spirit**, *he cannot enter into the kingdom of God.* What we can deduct from this rule, is that something metaphysical and unseen happens during baptism.

After baptism, it is time to begin the forty days fast, and I would like to reiterate, make sure to discuss your current health situation with your doctor before doing this. You should be of sound health before you do this! Next, you are going to use products like the ones I recommended in the earlier chapters. You need to make sure your body receives in liquid form: proteins, amino acids, folic acid, vitamins, and essential minerals for a safe forty-day fast.

During this time your body is going to begin to prepare for solar energy infusion. Your body will begin to make more melanocyte cells and convert your skin

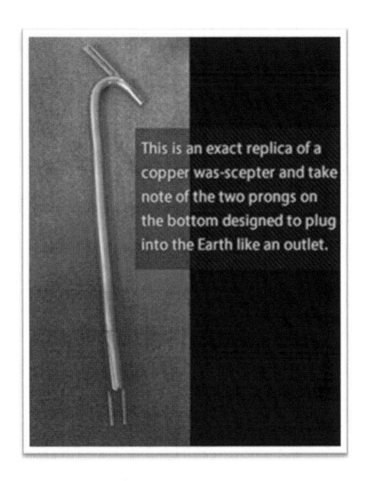

This is an exact replica of a copper was-scepter and take note of the two prongs on the bottom designed to plug into the Earth like an outlet.

into an upgraded solar panel. For the next forty days, you should Sun gaze during the "golden" hours, which are deemed less risky for eye damage. That is at sunrise to one hour after sunrise to one hour before sunset. As the ancients said, the Sun will send the human body "cake and ale" if your heart is perfected!

Also, read the Book of Proverbs and change your emotional thought process! I would recommend you pick a proverb and meditate on it as you Sun gaze. The commonly accepted Sungazing methodology is to Sungaze in ten-second increments every twenty-four hours. So, you would start out at 10 seconds day one and day two move on to 20 seconds, day three 30 seconds, etc.

You do this until you Sun gaze for a total of 45 minutes. The whole process takes nine months and brings a unique perspective to being born again, right? The optimal Sun gazing environment would be the beach where your whole body is exposed with the exception of covering up the private parts. You stand barefoot on the sand with the was-scepter in the right hand inserted into the Earth.

Your left-hand holds the ankh with the weak current pulsing through it while staring directly at the Sun. Remember the melanated skin is a proven superconductor of electromagnetic energy! Coupled with the low level of ultraviolet radiation through the optic nerve creates a trinity of energy coursing through the body. This brings a new perspective to being electrified!

During the 40 days fast your body is disconnecting from its reliance on material food to create energy. The body is now switching over to light energy, and the process is very similar to photosynthesis. You will also begin to gain spiritual senses as your signal raises in the "tree of life" in your brain. By the fourth day of fasting, hunger will leave your body, and your energy levels will normalize if you are taking the proper doses of the liquid products I recommended in an earlier chapter.

If you are feeling weak make sure you are taking the proper doses and remember without protein your body will begin to feed on muscle after fat stores are depleted. I also recommend monitoring your blood pressure daily during this time. After you complete your 40-day fast, you will still be Sun gazing because the entire plan is 273 days! You can return to solid food again but do it slowly.

Return to solid foods through bone broths and rice in order to ease into food again. There are some people who claim to no longer need solid food after reaching 273 days of successful sun-gazing. I do not believe you have to stop eating or the Most High would not have made pho soup so delicious! I am sure some people might attempt to see how long they can go without food or liquid supplements, but I strongly recommend you stay on the liquid products to stay healthy.

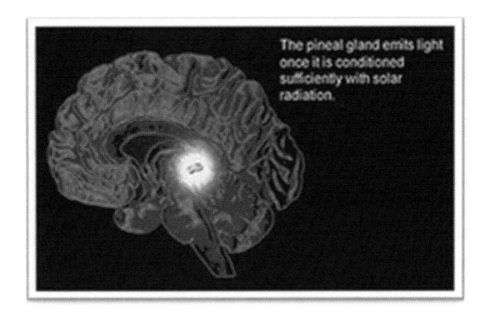

The pineal gland emits light once it is conditioned sufficiently with solar radiation.

Standing with the ankh and was-scepter while Sungazing will be a learning curve. We are returning to ancient ways that I believe involved the awakening of dormant DNA. Once the pineal gland reaches maturity, I believe it will light up because so many Renaissance painters captured this in their artwork. The pineal gland is bioluminescent, and it is right next to the "tree of life."

I wonder if the "tree of life" grows in the light? The Renaissance art earlier in the book shows a flame radiating out the heads of the Disciples. Science now understands that light can change DNA and DNA can conduct electrical current (Vijayender Bhalla, 2003). It is vital you drink mineralized water during this time and when you return to solid food choose healthy Sun grown food! The final state of Sun gazing is to have the solar dove enter the human body.

I believe you will be able to see into the spirit realm. While Sun gazing with the ankh and was-scepter you are using electromagnetism to activate your DNA to receive this solar dove. Do these "doves" facilitate the DNA transformation process? This is what we need to figure out because no one else has been able to replicate one miracle from ancient times.

In essence, the masses follow "anointed" men and women who cannot demonstrate any power that Jesus or His Disciples did. It is plain to all many churches are nothing more than businesses. True power is being in communication with the Throne and able to ask for the Power to heal someone and this power is sent through you. This is the path the book is discussing, and we know: baptism, prayer, meditation, and Sungazing is the way.

The 400-year curse on the Chosen People ends in 2019. Once the curse is lifted, the Chosen People must return to Him and His ways. I believe this book is the path to those ways. We cannot continue to rely on the

methodologies that have yielded negative results. Melanin is the catalyst to the gateway to another realm and the ancients celebrated this realm and left us blogs in stone for this very time.

Again, this is not Sun worship any more than using the Sun for a tan. It is a means to an end with spiritual properties we have yet to grasp. We are Children of the Light or also known as Children of the Sun. When the Lord said, "Let there be light" He designed it with a dual purpose. I believe the two terms "Light" and the "Sun" are interchangeable.

Once the Sun, ankh, and was-scepter aid in the completion of our dormant DNA transformation, we will be able to travel the Universe in spirit. Armed with this knowledge the Egyptian bas-relief walls and other hieroglyphics begin to take on a new meaning. The above picture can now decode as space/time bending as the ancient Egyptians travel through the wormhole to the Heavenly Kingdom. Again, we see the was-scepter and the ankh to travel 8.61 light years away in spirit, being led by through the Sun.

This is an astro-theology mimicking Jesus saying it is only through me to the Father. This is what we must return to as a people to escape the wicked rulers of this world. They have turned paradise into a cesspool of corruption and deceit which they exacerbate with mass murder. This is why we were cut off from the Heavenly Kingdom to stop us from accessing real power.

We are truly spiritual beings trapped in a human prison. Returning to the ancient ways is our only hope as people. This transformation makes us superhuman, and the wicked rulers of this Earth are afraid of this happening. I believe this is why mainstream entertainers are using ancient symbols to vilify them as evil. They are taking symbols once associated with our spiritual homeworld and promoting them as satanic.

For instance, the triangle is related to the Winter Triangle constellation; however, now the "Illuminati" are given an acknowledgment for it. Alternatively, a former crack dealer who goes by the name Jay Z is given credit for the ancient triangle symbol. None of this is true! If you study the Hebrew priest of Kohen you will see the triangle was part of the priestly blessing and some used it to direct the Sun to the pineal gland, while Sungazing.

I also believe the triangle was an homage to the Winter Triangle constellation where Renaissance painters depicted Heaven. As a result of living in the Information Age there needed to be a countermeasure on ancient knowledge, to curtail the masses from investigation. This is the reason why you see many occult symbols interwoven into an entertainer's performance art. These entertainers are adopting ancient symbols and artifacts to make them appear unholy, to discourage investigation.

The most abused ancient symbols are the triangle and the All-Seeing-Eye. After reading this book, you should be familiar with the original meaning for these symbols. Isaiah 5:20 (KJV) 20 *Woe unto them that call evil good, and good evil; that put darkness for light, and light for darkness; that put bitter for sweet, and sweet for bitter!* These entertainers attempt to deceive the masses by

Priest of Kohen used triangle for blessings and Sun gazing

vilifying ancient symbols pregnant with purpose. In truth, these entertainers are choosing darkness over the light.

These entertainers have become intoxicated with wealth and have chosen material over spiritual. Most of them will die unfulfilled without activating their spiritual selves. The hole most people feel in their souls is their spiritual bodies yearning to be activated. We all feel a tugging at our heartstrings to return to our original home and kingdom.

Therefore, the ancients were happy to be able to commune in both worlds. It is time we reevaluate those people who promote ancient things as evil. You know them because they have become obsessed with exposing darkness and offer no solutions. Well, I should not say that because many will sell you buckets of freeze dried food or coins with silver in them.

They are not searching for the righteous path because that leads to a total reliance on the Spirit and not the material. Many of these ancient symbols are interwoven into fashion and then worn by entertainers. The symbol gets vilified through association, and the observer will not study the origin of them out of fear. I believe these entertainers have handlers and the goal is to turn people away from them.

I heard some of the silliest commentaries regarding ancient symbols from the most far reaching observations. This YouTube commentator called the solar dove a "demon" coming out of the "Matrix" which was the Sun! People like this have no clue yet promote their opinions as authorities on things with an ancient origin. This is dangerous because it keeps people trapped in ignorance.

If you are following people like this, you will stay in the same place spiritually, and without change, you are wasting valuable time. It is my hope after reading this book you commit to the spiritual transformation process outlined by Jesus and the ancients. You also incorporate the ancient practice of Sun gazing into the process. I trust this ancient process will yield results.

You will then be a living spiritual example of what is possible in the world.

The Spirit's Power

1 Corinthians 2:4

"My message and my preaching were not with wise and persuasive words, but with a demonstration of the Spirit's power."

If you think about it, every mega church preacher relies on *wise* and *persuasive* words to pull you into their money pit. Mega preachers will tell you how wealthy the Lord wants you to be. Then they say, "If this message has touched you, then find it in your heart to donate to this ministry." Well, that is textbook persuasion.

None of these mega preachers can demonstrate one miracle Jesus *promised* us we could do. Nor have they activated themselves spiritually to demonstrate they know the path Jesus walked. Most of these church leaders today rely on *wise* words, which spiritually captivate their audience. The ancients were more hands-on with their spiritual development.

The Spirit is what comes out of the Sun, and the ancient symbol for the Spirit looks remarkably like the Christian dove. Jesus practiced the methodologies of conditioning Himself to receive the Spirit's power. This further substantiates the Eastern account of Jesus practicing Sun gazing. Once the Spirit enters the body, there is a DNA change which explains Jesus defying the laws of physics.

There is an understanding in Christian circles the Holy Spirit imbues the human recipient with abilities that describe as magical. Jesus demonstrated the ability to restore sight to a man who was born blind and the ability to walk to a disabled person. This is the first act of Jesus providing free healthcare! Jesus was able to "see" possessed people from afar and even raise the dead.

The Disciples were able to demonstrate the same. Nowadays the Christian masses follow men/women who cannot demonstrate one of these things Jesus or His Disciples did, yet they are leaders of the flocks. That was the entire point of this book was to travel back in time and reevaluate the beginning Age and the tools for spiritual transformation.

Today spirituality is an abject failure when it comes to demonstrating what the Disciples were able to do. It should be apparent to all we have missed a vital piece of the spiritual formula for transformation.

The definition of insanity is doing the same thing repeatedly and expecting a different result. Jesus was very clear when He said we would be able to do the same things He did.

In John 14:12, Jesus said, "*Verily, verily, I say unto you, He that believeth on me, the works that I do shall he do also; and greater works than these shall he do; because I go unto my Father.*" Jesus demonstrated the ability to change His molecular structure, become lighter than air, and walk on water. This is one example of the many abilities He gained through: baptism, prayer, water, and Sun gazing.

Although Jesus is part of the Godhead, He had to be born human to demonstrate what was possible in a human form. His body was still under the same laws of physics as ours until he put in the work and followed the formula for spiritual transformation. Jesus was not the first to do this either. Some portion of His central goal was to show humanity what the Pharisees covered up, to the individuals who might listen closely.

It was through demonstration He gained fame where ever he set foot, not because of His preaching. Jesus not only talked the talk, but he walked the walk, on water! Jesus and His Disciples were not alone in ancient history in demonstrating great abilities while in a human form. Moses was able to part the Red Sea, which I believe was from a power flowing through him.

It is important we understand that Jesus said in 1 Corinthians 2:4, "My message and my preaching were not with wise and persuasive words, **but with a demonstration of the Spirit's power**." You must agree preaching today is *devoid* of a demonstration of the Spirit's power! Why are we following people and supporting a church system that is a failure for two thousand years? After reading the previous chapters in this book you should conclude power will only be demonstrated after following His comprehensive path and that includes solar cultivation.

I have personally seen the "doves" that fly into and out of the Sun. I know they are real and they are not UFO because they have an ancient correlation to the Sun. We have seen them embodied in stone with the Assyrian Ashur pulling a bowstring with an arrow tipped with a dove-like object. This is what descended to the Earth and entered the body of Jesus.

I believe using the ankh and was-scepter magnetizes the human body to draw these "doves" inside the human body if the heart is perfected. This is what causes the dormant DNA to activate and where European scholars have erroneously labeled as Sun-gods. Can you imagine where the Earth would be if all of the people lived in peace and harmony? How advanced would this planet be if we stayed in contact with the Throne individually and collectively? This is why Jesus must come again to return the Earth to Universal harmony and the true teachings to humanity.

Before this happening, there will be a return to our ancient ways. The Holy Spirit's power can change our collective DNA. 2 Corinthians 5:17, states, " *17 Therefore, if anyone is in Christ, the new creation has come: The old has gone, the new is here*!" There is a mystery in this statement, and it involves a spiritual transformation.

It is more than just getting baptized, saying some words, or being nice when it suits you. There is an ancient methodology that must be followed to receive the Spirit's power. It is my belief the royal families hid the "keys of knowledge" from the common Egyptian people just as the Pharisees did. Therefore, some of them were considered gods. The royal families knew about the baptism, water, prayer, and the Sun gazing.

When it comes to Sun gazing dark skinned cultures had an advantage and perhaps greater power; for their ability to absorb sunlight was greater. Not all solar panels are equal, and there is a correlation between the number of solar panel cells and how much radiation can be absorbed. Therefore, it is important to wear a hooded linen tunic if your melanin stores are low.

This reminds me of Isaiah 9:6 (KJV) - *6 For unto us a child is born, unto us a son is given: and the government shall be upon his shoulder: and his name shall be called Wonderful, Counselor, The mighty God, The everlasting Father,* **The Prince of Peace**. The astro-theology substitutes the Sun for this role where the by-product of Sun gazing is a a great sense of peace and wellbeing. People could live in harmony and learn to express brotherly love. The challenge will be conditioning the heart and body to receive the Spirit.

The church system no longer believes it is possible to do the things Jesus demonstrated and they have abandoned hope of it. They make statements like, "Well, that was just Jesus, and we cannot expect to do what He did." Sadly, people have missed the point of Jesus incarnating into a human form. Jesus could have come to the Earth in Spirit, but He chose to be human to demonstrate what was possible while in a human form.

Meaning we have the potential to perform the very miracles, Jesus demonstrated if we seek Truth and follow His way. It is true the proverbial deck is stacked against us because we live in a system that curtails spiritual transformation. It is my hope this book will light the fire of exploration into these areas, and more people will receive the Holy Spirit. As it is now, people believe receiving the Holy Spirit is emotional alchemy without demonstration.

Jesus and His Disciples were able to demonstrate the great power, and that was part of His mission. Jesus taught a strict procedure that must be followed all together for the Spirit to enter the body. There are references to the rod and staff proving comfort, but these tools are never fully investigated or understood. How can a rod and staff comfort you? And now with Sun gazing it makes more sense.

We now know after reviewing the ancient Egyptian bas-relief and hieroglyphics the rod and the staff were used for Sun gazing. I have experienced the calming and peaceful effects of Sun gazing. The learning curve with the ankh will be using it in its current state or configuring it with a weak current less than 1 amp. Once the correct ankh configuration is test and evaluated, the human race can explore the process laid out before us by the ancients.

They were cultures who respected nature, making them naturalist. We live in the Information Age and Spirit has taken a backseat to artificial intelligence. Our Modern Age has replaced the spiritual world with the virtual world. Cell phones replaced telepathy, and we have become addicted to our technology devices. The ancients were the exact opposite and realized there was a Kingdom within us in the form of dormant DNA which could be awakened to travel the stars and return to the Heavenly Kingdom.

The modern church system understands we are a duality but lacks the keys of knowledge to our spiritual transformation. There are many well-intentioned pastors and preachers out there who strive to improve the lives of their flock. The common disconnect between these preachers and pastors is their training missed the true ancient path. The Vatican destroyed the true path taught by the ancients over centuries.

Hernán Cortés was a Spanish conquistador, or conqueror, best remembered for conquering the Aztec empire in 1521 and claiming Mexico for Spain. Soon after the conquering was done Jesuit priest showed up with the agenda of ferreting away spiritual secrets and science. We are at the mercy of 18th-century European academics that set the stage for an initial understanding of ancient Egypt, while much of their earliest research reflects prejudice, by jettisoning melanated case studies. Perhaps, if early European archeologist focused on the Sun and melanin connection in conjunction with the hieroglyphics, they would have unlocked spiritual cultivation methodologies.

Modern science understands melanin is a biological chemical molecule with amazing properties, and because of that, it makes sense why the ancient Egyptians wore kilts. Something the European man would not have been able to do exposed to extreme solar radiation. I say these things not to divide, but to emphasize not all the facts were laid out regarding the original ancient Egyptians. Therefore, it is imperative we rediscover and review ancient artifacts of what is hidden in plain view for the spiritual benefits for all humanity.

We need to start with a clean slate and I hope this is what this book can do. We should now see the Sun in a different light; no pun intended. Where we use the Sun as a tool for spiritual transformation; as did Jesus and many ancient cultures before him. In my opinion, it makes sense why the spiritual kingdom would send emissaries to Earth to retrain the masses in spiritual truths when they became lost.

We are not worshiping the Sun any more than someone who receives a tan from the Sun. The Sun is the great life sustainer in our solar system, and the ancient Egyptians knew it is also the great spiritual transformer. I would be remiss if I did not reemphasize the comprehensive process which includes a sloughing process regarding your mentality. If your mentality is not in line with the teachings of Jesus, you will not experience the transformation.

The process of being born again includes a releasing of everything you think you know and everything you currently are. Your sole expectation and emotional responses should be spiritual responses. If you are in a consistent state of conflict, you are not ready. If you are causing division, conflict, and non-righteously judging you are not ready.

Please remember many artists would paint Jesus pointing at His heart and then up. Your heart is not just pumping your blood, but it is the storehouse of your spiritual state. Your emotional state is the by-product of your ideology, to be born again, you must change your spiritual ideology to that of what Jesus taught.

This means operating out of the state of love, and that is easier said than done! If you are harboring behaviors, such as hatred, racism, oppression, manipulation, dishonesty, fraud, cheating, lying, jealousy, and sexual deviancy, you are out of sorts and will be unworthy to receive the Spirit. Let say you get to the finish line with the process and you retrain your heart, in addition to the: baptism, prayer, water, fasting, and sun-gazing. You may one day receive the Holy dove, and this also might be a question of the height of the terrain elevation where you are standing.

I trust after Sun gazing with the copper ankh, copper was-scepter, and following the strict ways of Jesus your dormant DNA will activate. The moment the Holy solar dove enters your body, you will be spiritually transformed. The signal in your "tree of life" will be raised to its highest potential and you will appear as a god to people. This might sound farfetched to some, but Psalm 82:6, states, "I have said, Ye are gods, and all of you are children of the Most High."

Unfortunately, most people stopped seeking truth because the answers are out there. We have so much power locked inside us; it had to be hidden to conquer our souls.

The Orion Kingdom

Job 38:31

"Can you bind the chains of the Pleiades, Or loose the cords of Orion?"

Before I delve into this chapter, I would like to preface it by saying many other writers have produced fascinating works on Orion. I hope to build upon them and discuss some of the academics, archeologist, and independent researchers who indelibly carried on the legacy of ancient Egypt discovery. My main objective here is to build a plausible case that behind the physical veil Orion is the vast Spiritual Kingdom. Our current technology cannot observe or measure this Kingdom, but we do have a diverse collection of near-death accounts of people who have experienced this Kingdom in spirit.

I will respectfully begin with the physical observations of ancient Egypt, Sirius, the Pleiades constellation and Orion before I segue into the spiritual case Orion is where the Kingdom of Heaven is located. I will remind you before beginning the (Santini, 2010) Golden and Silver gate, the respective anciently

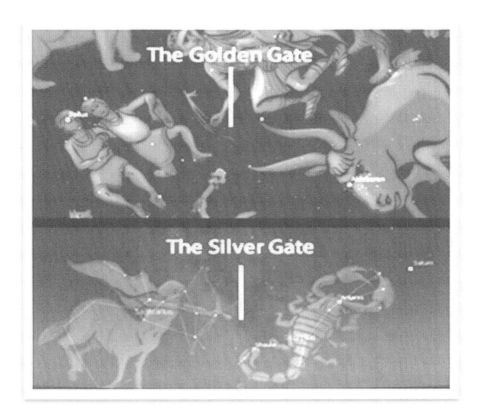

acknowledged entrance and exit to Heaven are both located *in* Orion. All roads in various ancient cultures have origin stories that begin in Orion. This is where I believe the Most High became conscious and constructed all things in Spirit *first*.

The duality of this construction means the physical world is the by-product of the spiritual world. At the beginning of the 20th century, Gerald Massey released *Ancient Egypt: The Light of the World*, where he submitted Egypt birthed the human civilization and was the foundation for Jewish and Christian beliefs. Gerald Massey, even went against the grain from some of his white supremacist contemporaries; who steadfastly denied ancient Egypt was the birth of a highly melanated people. In 1852, when the American diplomat Bayard Taylor (1825-1878) visited Sudan and gazed upon the temple carvings of sumptuously clad gods and rulers with clearly African features, he also found it inconceivable that they could have been created by black-skinned people.

Massey stated in his book, "*The dignity is so ancient that the insignia of the Pharaoh evidently belonged to the time when Egyptians wore nothing but the girdle of the Negro.*" This means Massey was aware of the melanin connection after being immersed in ancient Egyptian artifacts. Massey believed ancient Egypt was the beginning of the human race and that lends credence to the African woman's mitochondrial DNA, as the mother to all human genetics on the Earth today. It also lends credence that melanin was a tool for spiritual transformation, based on what science knows of melanin today.

The ancients embodied in stone artifacts illustrating the: pineal gland, the Sun, and entwined snakes illustrating DNA. These components were part of the ancient formula for transitioning to the realm of spirit. It is said we are spiritual beings having a human experience and the ancient Egyptians also operated out of full duality. Meaning part of their historical archives are about physical things while the other is about spiritual experiences.

The spiritual perspective has been over-looked because of being analyzed without spiritual goggles. If Massey understood the ancient Egyptians could travel in the spirit realm (while living), I am sure he would have had a volume three to his masterpiece. Traveling in the spiritual realm also adds an explanation to the bizarre hybrid humanoid characters illustrated in hieroglyphics and bas-reliefs.

In fact, these are the same type of beings encountered by people who experimented with (DMT) dimethyltryptamine. DMT is a naturally occurring psychedelic compound of the tryptamine family. It instigates a very quick and extremely powerful psychedelic experience. Every night you go to bed your brain releases a dose of DMT from the pineal gland and you enter the dream state consequently when you die your body receives a massive dose of DMT.

This DMT chemical releases the subconscious mind to what we call the "dream world" but it is really the spirit world. Because it is small does the human consciousness stays tethered to the human body. Upon death, a massive dose of DMT releases which severs the connection to the material world (Strassman, 2000). Again, we have the pineal gland playing another role in the otherworldly experience of humans.

I would like to reiterate the pineal gland is responsible for releasing a chemical to allow the human soul to leave the body in spirit and a massive dose of DMT at death. The ancient Egyptians were said to be obsessed with the afterlife, but they were in communication with the spirit realm while living, as well. How did the ancients know the relationship between our Sun and Sirius? DMT research certainly provides a fascinating insight into the spirit realm.

Who educated the ancients on cosmic things? Where did the ancient Egyptians learn specifications for building the pyramids and the methodologies for constructing them? Many researchers would like to build a case for ancient aliens, but the Bible has examples of sending blueprints from the Heavenly Kingdom to men conditioned to receive the messages.

Noah received exact specifications for building the Ark in the Bible.

Ancient-alien believers rarely if ever consider a connection to ancient architecture and the inclusion of the Divine Mind. The Book of Genesis includes a narrative where Noah received special instructions from another realm by what he understood as God Himself. Below is the Genesis account of Noah, where he receives instructions from a non-earthly source.

Genesis 6:8-22 (KJV)

8 But Noah found grace in the eyes of the Lord.9 These are the generations of Noah: Noah was a just man and perfect in his generations, and Noah walked with God. 10 And Noah begat three sons, Shem, Ham, and Japheth. 11 The earth also was corrupt before God, and the earth was filled with violence. 12 And God looked upon the earth, and, behold, it was corrupt; for all flesh had corrupted his way upon the earth. 13 And God said unto Noah, The end of all flesh is come before me; for the earth is filled with violence through them; and, behold, I will destroy them with the earth. 14 Make thee an ark of gopher wood; rooms shalt thou make in the ark, and shalt pitch it within and without with pitch. 15 And this is the fashion which thou shalt make it of: The length of the ark shall be three hundred cubits, the breadth of it fifty cubits, and the height of it thirty cubits. 16 A window shalt thou make to the ark, and in a cubit shalt thou finish it above;and the door of the ark shalt thou set in the side thereof; with lower, second, and third stories shalt thou make it. 17 And, behold, I, even I, do bring a flood of waters upon the earth, to destroy all flesh, wherein is the breath of life, from under heaven; and everything that is in the earth shall die. 18 But with thee will I establish my covenant; and thou shalt come into the ark, thou, and thy sons, and thy wife, and thy sons' wives with thee. 19 And of every living thing of all flesh, two of every sort shalt thou bring into the ark, to keep them alive with thee; they shall be male and female. 20 Of fowls after their kind, and of cattle after their kind, of *every creeping thing of the earth after his kind, two of every sort shall come unto thee, to keep them alive. 21 And take thou unto thee of all food that is eaten, and thou shalt gather it to thee; and it shall be for food for thee, and for them. 22 Thus did Noah; according to all that God commanded him, so did he.*

This is an example of the Most High providing the intellectual property before the implementation of the labor phase or in other words project management. This is not the only example of this happening in the Bible. It happens again with Moses, and he too receives Divine specifications, this time for the design of the Ark of the Covenant. Once the instructions were followed the product met the quality assurance of the Most High and it was utilized by the priest. We see this example with Moses in the Book of Exodus.

Exodus 25:8-40 (KJV)

8 And let them make me a sanctuary; that I may dwell among them. 9 According to all that I shew thee, after the pattern of the tabernacle, and the pattern of all the instruments thereof, even so shall ye make it. 10 And they shall make an ark of shittim wood: two cubits and a half shall be the length thereof, and a cubit and a half the breadth thereof, and a cubit and a half the height thereof. 11 And thou shalt overlay it with pure gold, within and without shalt thou overlay it, and shalt make upon it a crown of gold round about. 12 And thou shalt cast four rings of gold for it and put them in the four corners thereof; and two rings shall be in the one side of it, and two rings in the other side of it. 13 And thou shalt make staves of shittim wood and overlay them with gold. 14 And thou shalt put the staves into the rings by the sides of the ark, that the ark may be borne with them. 15 The staves shall be in the rings of the ark: they shall not be taken from it. 16 And thou shalt put into the ark the testimony which I shall give thee. 17 And thou shalt make a mercy seat of pure gold: two cubits and a half shall be the length thereof, and a cubit and a half the breadth *thereof. 18 And thou shalt make two cherubims of gold, of beaten work shalt thou make them, in the two ends of the mercy seat. 19 And make one cherub on the one end, and the other cherub on the other end: even of the mercy seat shall ye make the cherubims on the two ends thereof. 20 And the cherubims shall stretch forth their wings on high, covering the mercy seat with their wings, and their faces shall look one to another; toward the mercy seat shall the faces of the cherubims be. 21 And thou shalt put the mercy seat above upon the ark; and in the ark thou shalt put the testimony that I shall give thee. 22 And there I will meet with thee, and I will commune with thee from above the mercy seat, from between the two cherubims which are upon the ark of the testimony, of all things which I will give thee in commandment unto the children of Israel. 23 Thou shalt also make a table of shittim wood: two cubits shall be the length thereof, and a cubit the breadth thereof, and a cubit and a half the height thereof. 24 And thou shalt* overlay it with pure gold and make thereto a crown of gold round about. 25 And thou shalt make unto it a border of an hand breadth round about, and thou shalt make a golden crown to the border thereof round about. 26 And thou shalt make for it four rings of gold,and put the rings in the four corners that are on the four feet thereof. 27 Over against the border shall the rings be for places of the staves to bear the table. 28 And thou shalt make the staves of shittim wood, and overlay them with gold, that the table may be borne with them. 29 And thou shalt make the dishes thereof, and spoons thereof, and covers thereof, and bowls thereof, to cover withal: of pure gold shalt thou make them. 30 And thou shalt set upon the table shewbread before me always. 31 And thou shalt make a candlestick of pure gold: of beaten work shall the candlestick be made: his shaft, and his branches, his bowls, his knops, and his flowers, shall be of the same. 32 And six branches shall come out of the sides of it; three branches of the candlestick *out of the one side, and three branches of the candlestick out of the other side: 33 Three bowls made like unto almonds, with a knop and a flower in one branch; and three bowls made like almonds in the other branch, with a knop and a flower: so in the six branches that come out of the candlestick. 34 And in the candlesticks shall be four bowls made like unto almonds, with their knops and their flowers. 35 And there shall be a knop under two branches of the same, and a knop under two branches of the same, and a knop under two branches of the same, according to the six branches that proceed out of the candlestick. 36 Their knops and their branches shall be of the same: all it shall be one beaten work of pure gold. 37 And thou shalt make the seven lamps thereof: and they shall light the lamps thereof, that they may give light over against it. 38 And the tongs thereof, and the snuff dishes thereof, shall be of pure gold. 39 Of a talent of pure gold shall he make it, with all these vessels. 40 And*

look that thou make them after their pattern,
which had shewed thee in the mount.

Yet, another case of The Most High providing highly detailed specifications to another human from the spiritual realm to the physical realm. It is also fascinating the Ark of the Covenant design was for the Most High to *dwell* inside and begs the question...how? How do you house the omnipotent Creator in a box? Or was this more of a communication device between worlds?

What we do know for sure is Universal knowledge was shared from the Heavenly Kingdom with men on the Earth, and every theory should include this instead of just ancient aliens! Why did the ancient Egyptians mark the Sirius star for the flooding of the Nile and their New Year? Is there a connection between near-death-experience and traveling to Orion? I believe there is an inverse duality between the black hole and the tunnel of white light near-death-people travel.

What we see in the physical is black, but in spirit, these people see a white tunnel of light as they travel to the Orion Kingdom, 8.611 light years above the Earth. There is an interesting Biblical scripture where Isaiah

55:8-9 (NIV), states, 8 "For my thoughts are not your thoughts, neither are your ways my ways," declares the Lord. 9 "**As the heavens are higher than the earth**, so are my ways higher than your ways and my thoughts than your thoughts. Many of the ancient Egyptian hieroglyphs illustrated Sirius including the bas-relief walls.

As time progressed the Vatican took ownership of the Sirius mystery and it changed to an emphasis on the Winter Triangle constellation. Orion is mentioned in the Bible four times not just because it is the most storied part of the Universe, but I believe is where the Heavenly Kingdom is in Spirit. Many other ancient creation myths are located in Orion. The Mayan's *Popul Vuh* is their cultures story of Creation, and it too is based in Orion. The ancients appeared to universally accept Orion as the origin of the dwelling of the Supreme Intelligence.

Of all the inconceivable vast real estate in the Universe, why is there such diverse ancient cultural focus on Orion and Pleiades? These star systems have consistently illustrated through ancient artifacts. The ancients taught this is the home of Creation and all things living. I believe at times angels were confused with gods and the Book of Enoch speaks of angels who descended to Earth.

These angels considered "fallen" because they left their original habitat which must be Orion. Jude 1:6, *"And the angels which kept not their first estate, but left their own habitation, he hath reserved in everlasting chains under darkness unto the judgment of the great day."* There are two anciently revered transit points in space known as the "Golden" and "Silver Gate." The "Golden" gate is between the Sagittarius and Scorpio constellation, and the "Silver" gate is between the Gemini and Taurus constellation.

The ancients stated the "Golden" gate is where celestial beings would enter Heaven. The ancients stated the "Silver" gate is where the celestial beings would exit the Heavens. Both the "Golden" and the "Silver" gate locate in opposite points in Orion. Heaven having two gateways was a belief universally accepted in ancient times captured by the: magi, monks, mystics, philosophers, poets, prophets, priests, and embodied across various ancient cultures in stone artifacts.

I think the most noted relationship to the "Silver" gate is the reference to the "Pearly Gates." These are spiritual transition points in Orion, and they can only be seen in spirit. Science has progressively matured to the understanding of invisible matter makes up most of the Universe. Science cannot observe this matter, and they only can identify it by its gravitational effects.

There is so much we do not know, but most of humanity rest assured that Spirit is not real and nothing more than a product of Faith. The ancients left enough symbols engrained in stone to leave modern man clues on a formula to unlock the duality of man. There are modern dutiful and unheralded researchers building on the researchers of the past. Years ago, I learned of a (Wilten, 2012) book titled, "Orion in the Vatican" by Danny Wilten.

He is an unheralded independent researcher building upon the legacy of many Vatican personalities and Egyptian archeologist from the seventeenth and eighteenth centuries. In his book, he analyzed Vatican paintings which appeared to have an overlay with the Orion Nebula. My takeaway was Renaissance artist were Divinely inspired and painted elements of the Orion Nebula in their paintings. Wilten used a Photoshop technique that presented very convincing cases.

The Egyptian Book of the Dead, The Pyramid Texts, The Holy Bible, Mayan Popol Vuh, Corpus Hermeticum, The Kybalion, alchemical drawings by the masters such as Athanasius Kircher, Theosophy, Gnosis, were used as a pretext to build a case that Vatican artist included the Orion Nebula in their works. This ancient knowledge was shared with the high-level priest, Jesuits, and royalty who were deemed worthy of these secrets. There is another researcher I came across who studied ancient cultures and star constellations relationship to ancient cultures. His name is Wayne Herschel, and he submits ancient aliens brought civilization to the Earth. (Herschel, 2003)

This theory is not without merit because the Book of Enoch claims this very thing with the difference these are spiritual beings. It is no secret in the Bible the Most High created another race of beings before the human race. They too can be considered "aliens" but were choirs of angels that lived in the spiritual realm with the Most High. However, these angels could appear as human, and you would not know the difference.

This is the area I differ from many independent researchers because they do not consider the plausibility of an advanced life form as spiritual.

Herschel also notes the Taurus constellation as a focal point embodied in stone and worshiped by ancient cultures. This is remarkable because the Taurus constellation is part of the "Silver Gate" which is where celestially beings were witnessed exiting Heaven. Where Herschel and I are fundamentally different is I believe these are spiritual beings, while he believes they are "aliens."

At times I am miffed because archeology has provided the Earth with a rich spiritual history. We also have evidence our Sun is the catalyst for great spiritual transformation in the human body. I believe our Sun is connected to the Sirius star and this is where the Heavenly Kingdom is located. Our Sun was created by the Most High with a great number of benefits to all life on Earth and the biggest secret is it can awaken sleeping DNA in the human body.

At the end of the day, I tip my hat to both of these independent researchers because they are continuing the legacy of unlocking ancient secrets by their diligent predecessors. On the following page, there is an ancient Egyptian bas-relief with the Sun and the Sirius star represented. The 11:11 on the bottom has a special meaning to me. In 2001, I began to see 11:11 on clocks

so frequently it became a mystery to me as to why. I even fought back and avoided clocks an hour before and it began to manifest in other ways.

It would appear on a receipt as 11:11 in change or I would hear that number on the news. I studied the

Mayan, December 21, 2012, prophecy since the mid-1990s. I was stunned to find out December 21, 2012, end of Age, would happen exactly at 11:11 Universal Time, which is time-based on the Earth's rotation and relationship to the center of the galaxy. After seeing the previous picture of the bas-relief, I now believe I was led to the Sun and Sirius.

I realized this when I saw 11:11 under the Sun, leading to the Sirius star. The human race was born in Orion in spirit first and merged into the material world through the birth process. Upon death, man will leave the material world and return to Orion in spirit. The Bible also states in Amos 5:8 (KJV) - *8 Seek him that maketh the seven stars and Orion, and turneth the shadow of death into the morning, and maketh the day dark with night: that calleth for the waters of the sea, and poureth them out upon the face of the earth: The Lord is his name.*

This verse is more than just beautiful poetry but another plug for the Pleiades constellation and Orion. Studying near-death-experience of people who went to Heaven have common and uncommon characteristics. The most common is traveling through a white tunnel and greeted by former loved ones who previously died.

There is a feeling of overwhelming peace and love. Some see a magnificent gate and others see different levels of Heaven, while some even meet Jesus.

Heaven describes as being architecturally amazing with living stones, waters, trees, and crystals as the elemental constructs. Even the colors in Heaven describe as being more vibrant, and even indescribable new colors. Could Orion be a veil for the Heavenly Kingdom? Orion must be in another dimension outside the observable physical dimension, like dark matter.

Orion is far too discussed in ancient civilizations at the beginning of Creation and must be the Kingdom of the Most High. It is very difficult to leave you with tangible evidence in this chapter because these are spiritual things we are discussing. Finally, it is the ancient civilizations that embodied a star in stone more than 8.611 light years from Earth and it must be more than just a star.

I can only surmise this Sirius star was taught to them by spiritual beings, much like the story of the Dogon Tribe in Africa. The Dogon oral history states amphibious beings landed in a ship from space and taught them about the Sirius star, and at the time invisible companion stars, long before modern technology could even detect it! A book was written about the Dogon's fascinating knowledge! (Temple, 1998)

The most descriptive account of the Heavenly Kingdom I am aware of is from Enoch. He provided eyewitness testimony of Heavenly places, characters, and mechanics of the Kingdom. The most stunning prophecy from the Book of Enoch is that the Holy One will leave His dwelling and appear on Earth! The Most High will descend to Mount Sinai with His Holy Ones in a display of unimaginable power.

There is a great earthquake associated with this remarkable event; I often wonder if this event is related to Revelation 6:12, because it will be a great earthquake? Revelation 6:12 (KJV) *12 And I beheld when he had opened the sixth seal, and, lo, there was a great earthquake; and the sun became black as sackcloth of hair, and the moon became as blood;*

The Bible states souls chose to incarnate on Earth lending credence to the plausibility the human race begins and returns to spirit. The Book of Enoch also addresses distinct beings which have Heavenly responsibilities, such as, the Watchers, the Holy Ones, war angels, and the rebel angels. Enoch communicated with both sets of these beings and both acknowledged the authority of the Most High. While Enoch was interacting with spiritual beings he was nowhere to be found on the Earth.

The Book of Enoch does not explain how Enoch was able to leave the physical realm and transition to spirit. What it does suggest is that the human body can enter the spiritual realm and return to the physical realm. Enoch was considered righteous which means he "followed the path of the ancient way" to the Heavenly Kingdom. My point is Enoch was "born again" and in my opinion practiced the things Jesus required us to do; in addition to Sun gazing. The Book of Enoch also suggests spiritual beings can transition to physical matter.

The Throne Room of the Most High must be unimaginably gigantic because Enoch said there were 100,000,000 million spiritual beings surrounding the Most High. If we attempt to scale this spiritual crowd to an earthly crowd, we can speculate the size of the Throne Room. For this example, I will use the 2009 crowd size for former President Obama's inauguration. The above picture shows 1.8 million people in the crowd and you can see the volume here.

Now imagine almost one hundred times this volume of spiritual beings surrounding the Most High in the Throne Room! The Orion Nebula is a gigantic storied region of space which certainly could house a gazillion of beings. In my opinion, Enoch proved the spirit realm dwarfed the physical realm when he stated, "*And the dwelling of the Spirits of Heaven is Heaven, but the dwelling of the spirits of the Earth, who were born on the Earth, is Earth.*"

If we compare this verse to Jeremiah 1:5 you will see all human life begins in spirit: Jeremiah 1:5, states, 5 *"Before I formed you in the womb I knew[a] you, before you were born I set you apart; I appointed you as a prophet to the nations.*" The Orion-to-Earth connection must be a system created by the Most High for the evolution of the soul. This is why the ancients included Orion in their oral histories and artifacts. Enoch witnessed the Watchers transitioning from a spiritual fire state to that of a human.

Solar Prophecy

Malachi 4:2 - 2

But unto you that fear my name shall the Sun of righteousness arise with healing in his wings, and ye shall go forth and grow up as calves of the stall.

The transformative powers of the Sun on the human body are amazing. It seems everything created by the Most High has duality, and this must include the Sun. I presented a case of the Sun's dual effect on spiritual cultivation. Most people understand the Sun can give you a tan, but how many know the effect on the human spirit? I will tell you not many!

One of the least discussed prophecies in the Bible regards the Sun. Hollywood addressed this prophecy in the movie, *Knowing,* starring Nicholas Cage. This movie addressed the prophetic book of Malachi 4:1, where it states, *"4 For, behold, the day cometh, that shall burn as an oven; and all the proud, yea, and all that do wickedly, shall be stubble: and the day that cometh shall burn them up, saith the Lord of hosts, that it shall leave them neither root nor branch."* This movie showcased the destruction of the Earth via a massive coronal mass ejection. The Sun burned the Earth like a marshmallow in a bonfire, and the silver lining was angels saved some of the children of the Earth. Even Hopi have a prophecy of this world burned by fire. (Staff I. C., 2017)

This prophecy is not all bad because this solar event is prophesied to transform DNA. This solar event speaks of a moment in time where the Sun will *heal* the righteous and *burn* the wicked. The Hebrew word for righteous is *tsadiya,* and it means "straight path." After reading the previous chapters, I believe this "straight path" is self-explanatory. It cannot hurt solar conditioning is part of this path.

The Hebrew word for wicked is *rasha,* and it means "departing" from the path to God. Now imagine how many people departed from the path to God. When Oprah was marketing New Age philosophy on her titular talk show, she said, "There are many paths to the Light." Now you know there are not many paths but there is a formula of a loving heart and then the solar conversion methodologies discussed in the previous chapters. Oprah was oblivious to the role of the Sun because of the logical emotional alchemy presented by a stable of New Age authors she promoted.

I will never forget what Eckhart Tolle said on her show when Oprah asked him, "What do you think happens after death?" Eckhart Tolle, replied, "I don't think about it." The irony is Eckhart Tolle is heralded as a spiritual guru, yet he is oblivious to the spiritual world witnessed by the ancients; not mention Eckhart Tolle cannot demonstrate one thing the Disciples did. Our whole capitalist system is a prison, designed to cause solar malnutrition and if Lucifer is real, this timeless being has led most of the world astray.

Who of us have time to view the sunrise or sunset and sun gaze? Collectively the average human has no time to be solar conditioned, and I believe this tie to the "Day of the Lord" outlined in the Book of Malachi. I believe this "healing" from the Sun's rays will awaken sleeping DNA and there will be an instantaneous change to the human physiology. This "healing" will also cause a feeling of euphoria in people who get healed by the Sun.

The "Great Day of the Lord" in Biblical prophecy also has a destructive component as well to the Earth. Although it appears many will suffer destructio there are some people who will survive. Those who do survive will experience tremendous euphoria.

The Great Day of the Lord

4 1 "For behold, the day is coming, burning like an oven, when tall the arrogant and tall evildoers will be stubble. The day that is coming shall set them ablaze, says the Lord of hosts, so that it will leave them neither root nor branch. 2 But for you who fear my name, the sun of righteousness shall rise with healing in its wings. You shall go out leaping like calves from the stall. 3 And you shall tread down the wicked, for they will be ashes under the soles of your feet, on the day when I act, says the Lord of hosts. 4 b "Remember the law of my servant Moses, the statutes and rules 2 that I commanded him at Horeb for all Israel.5 d "Behold, I will send you Elijah the prophet before the great and awesome day of the Lord comes. 6 And he will turn the hearts of fathers to their children and the hearts of children to their fathers, lest I come and strike the land with a decree of   utter destruction."3

It is plausible that following the methodologies outlined by Jesus and sun gazing with the ankh/was-scepter conditions you to survive the Day of the Lord?

Can the Sun differentiate between who is righteous and who is wicked? If so how would the Sun measure the man? This is why I believe when you are "born again" you actually become Sun worthy as well through the process outlined in this book.

There is another prophecy that speaks about the Sun and the power of the Sun on this day is almost unimaginable. Isaiah 30:26 states, **the Earth will receive seven days of sunshine in one day**. This must be connected to Malachi 4:1-6 and that amount of radiation will certainly pass through walls so even if you are not outside the rays will find you. Meaning there is no escaping the consequences of this event.

The Sun's ultraviolet (UV) light consists of radiation acting as an agent that causes mutations in DNA. The exposure to ultraviolet light causes endocrine chemical changes altering the shape of DNA. This is a double-edged sword because it could correct the DNA's shape or damage DNA code. Skin cancer is the outcome of DNA damage to the skin after prolonged exposure to the Sun. In an earlier chapter, I presented the human body increases melanin production when fasting and melanin protects the human body from excessive solar radiation.

In my opinion, removing solar conditioning from spiritual cultivation turned the masses away from the "straight path." The Sun conditions the human body to create feel-good chemicals and even the Day of the Lord will cause a "healing" in the human body, with massive feel-good chemicals. Have you seen a calf released from a stall? If not type into YouTube, "calf released from a stall" and watch them go buck wild!

Does it not make sense to condition the human body safely using the Sun as a tool? I believe there is a misunderstanding when it comes to Pre-Tribulation perception and this connection is to the Sun. Matthew 24:40 states, "*Then shall two be in the field; the one shall be taken, and the other left.*" The misconception is the righteous will be taken, but how can the righteous be healed on the Day of the Lord if they are not on Earth? The wicked (those who left the straight path) will be the ones taken off the Earth through a fiery death process.

On the Day of the Lord, the wicked will be burn to ashes! There is also another Scripture that proves the Believers will be on the Earth for the Second Coming. 1 Thessalonians 4:17, states, "*Then we which are alive and remain shall be caught up together with them in the clouds, to meet the Lord in the air: and so shall we ever be with the Lord.*" In order to qualify for this verse, you have to be alive and on Earth to be caught up in the clouds.

The food supply is poisoned with chemicals as is the drinking water supply. Diseases like cancer are on the upswing and is trace to the food supply coupled with a lack of solar illumination in the human body. There are even pesticides which feminize the human body. There should be no question about the combination of processed food and water is damaging human DNA and the Day of the Lord will cure this.

Isaiah 13:10, states, "*For the stars of the heavens and their constellations will not give their light; the sun will be dark at its rising, and the moon will not shed its light.*" This is another solar-related prophecy managing our expectations the Earth will be in a state of darkness. Furthermore, this means the Earth would begin to reduce in temperature. An excellent model for this would be the 30 days of night in Alaska. These are all survivable events on the Earth, but those who veer off the straight path will experience the cold sting of death.

As you can see one of the least discussed prophecies in the Bible concerns the Sun. Most people are well aware of the Sun's role regarding life on the

Earth. Most people understand the Earth's distance from the Sun changes the seasons. What most people do not understand is the effects of ultraviolet A and ultraviolet B on the human body.

As the ozone layer is depleted stronger concentrations of (PINKSTONE, 2018) ultraviolet A and ultraviolet B beam through to the Earth. Scientific studies have used plant models to study the effects of this increasing ultraviolet radiation. The photosynthesis process was damaged and there was evidence of the inactivation of the light-harvesting complex. When it comes to the human body we have defenses. The human body can create more melanin cells by fasting and direct sunlight.

Our melanin cells can absorb ultraviolet A and ultraviolet B radiation and turn this radiation into energy. It appears of all life on the planet; humanity is best suited to survive the Day of the Lord. Studies have shown a lower incidence of skin cancer in individuals with more concentrated melanin, i.e. darker skin tone. What is alarming being skin cancer rates are on the rise with the expectation 112,000 new cases by 2030. (Simon, 2015)

The solar prophecy of the Day of the Lord includes a direct reference to solar rays. Isaiah 30:26, speaks of the Sun shining like seven suns in one day. This is an unimaginable amount of ultraviolet A and ultraviolet B radiation beamed to the Earth! It would be advisable for all human life to avoid the Sun on this day; especially those with lower amounts of melanin. Therefore, I believe Sun gazing is a physical and spiritual conditioning necessity.

It allows the body to become conditioned for greater amounts of ultraviolet A and ultraviolet B radiation. If I am correct in my assessments of the ancient artifacts there will be a DNA change, and perhaps this is the protection from death on the Day of Lord? Is it not ironic the Most High uses the Sun to activate humanities spiritual self and to destroy those who do not use it? The Sun has one of the hugest roles in prophecy, and in my experience, the least discussed in the church system.

There is also a connection between the Sirius star and our Sun. We see this illustrated in Renaissance artwork, especially by Athanasius Kircher. Even if this connection is in Spirit, it is still a connection. *If God is the bringer of life (energy) and light, Sirius fits the description, it transmits its energy (highly charged particles) to our entire system via the magnetic field lines. We literally receive energy from Sirius! Did the ancient priests understand this process, thus naming this star "God"?* (Denis, 2001)

Conclusion

Proverbs 4:18

*The path of the righteous is like the morning sun,
shining ever brighter till the full light of day.*

We live in a time where the teachings of Jesus are: profited from, twisted, misunderstood, and bastardized with political agendas. I heard radio personalities leading their cult following blabbering about the "spiritual war" while fighting for their "gun rights" and "freedom of speech." While democracy and liberty are certainly important cornerstones for the pursuit of happiness, they are not part of the power of the Spirit demonstrated by Jesus. The life of Jesus was a demonstration of power in human form by Spirit.

1 Corinthians 2:4 (NIV) - *4 My message and my preaching were not with wise and persuasive words, but with a demonstration of the Spirit's power.* Is there anyone we listen too or financially empower as "men of God" that can demonstrate one power of the Spirit? Sure, many of them know some Scripture, but most use it out of context and mislead their cult. Once you

understood Jesus also came to Earth to demonstrate what was capable through the human body, you will abandon these powerless pastors, preachers, priest, and self-appointed "Watchmen."

The keys of knowledge were hidden centuries ago, and we were born into a spiritual prison of half-truths. Jesus showed us a formula, and the Catholic Church owned the repository of this truth and suppressed it. Once men learned to profit off half-truths and misdirection the "straight path" is hidden. If this path has not been hidden how come no one can demonstrate the power of the Spirit?

I have spoken to some stated they have cast out demons and performed healings, but never have I heard any similar to Biblical accounts. Where men were born blind, and then became able to see, or people cripple from birth were given the ability to walk, by the power of the Spirit. These are Biblical events demonstrating the Spirit, and to my knowledge, no one on Earth has been able to achieve this power. Albert Einstein said, *"The definition of insanity is doing the same thing over and over again but expecting different results."*

Who can the masses depend on to share authentic spiritual teachings, which yield demonstratable results?

We have prosperity preachers who own million-dollar homes and private jets, yet they cannot demonstrate the power of the Spirit. We have other radio personalities who mix conspiracy theories from "secret sources" with cherry-picked spiritual teachings, and they too profit by pandering for donations for their powerless ministries. They use fear tactics to drive you into predefined sales pitches, and all of them rely on "wise and persuasive words."

I have heard some of them admit they do this because their followers are stupid. None of this is part of the "straight path," and that is the true first order at hand. If it were not for ancient artifacts and other ancient narratives, we would not be able to piece the straight path together. The Bible is not the only source of truth in the ancient world. Ancient Egyptian proverbs source the Book of Proverbs by thousands of years yet speak the same truth.

Jesus incarnated on the Earth to demonstrate what was once universally known, but subsequently hidden from the people. How did this happen? There are several reasons for this which can be attributed to cataclysms, religious omission, and a conspiracy to keep mankind ignorant of his true nature. What would be the point of this conspiracy?

Well, it would separate humanity from direct contact with the Heavenly Kingdom and bind it to the material world. Have you noticed each year America is turning more and more into a strip club? The Catholic Church is famous for creating the Priest as an intercessor for their followers. Jesus did not teach we need an intercessor and taught us to pray directly to the Most High.

Have you noticed many Christians believe they are on point with the teachings of Jesus? They know all of the catchphrases like:

- Are you saved?
- Are you born again?
- Are you baptized?
- Do you speak in tongues?
- I don't want to judge.

They share their Faith with great hubris because at the end of the day they cannot demonstrate anything on a Biblical scale. It should be apparent something is missing from our modern understanding of spiritual cultivation. Jesus taught His Disciples to do amazing things and promised us we could do the same. Why are

Christians so confident they have the Holy Spirit when they cannot demonstrate what other Biblical figures did who demonstrated it?

It is the very ideology of the modern Christian that is the great conundrum. Over the years I immersed myself into online Christian groups and experienced firsthand the psychosis plaguing their minds. Some blather about love until they disagree and then the claws come out. While others claim everything, you need is the Bible, yet the Vatican tampered with the original practices, and Jesus was upset with the Pharisees for *hiding* the *keys of knowledge.* When exactly did the Pharisees return these keys?

The most important psychosis is the belief in a process that has yielded zero tangible capabilities. The people are divided by race, social economics, and now an array of newly defined political platforms. Divide and conquer has been augmented by the art of collective distraction. Meanwhile, the Sun beams down on a people oblivious to their connection to the Sun.

The ancients left us clues embodied in stone which could not be hidden or easily removed. The reoccurring themes throughout many different ancient cultures were the Sun, the pineal gland, and DNA. How they learned this is another mystery, but if they were in contact with the Heavenly realms, therein lies the answer. As modern science and technology close the gaps of understanding between ancient practices and modern perspectives, we see not just reason, but a system.

This system is very similar to photosynthesis but has much more complex requirements to "flower" for humanity. Sun gazing seems to be the missing link in a relationship with the example left by Jesus. Although Jesus is mentioned in ancient India religious texts many will dismiss it as a false doctrine. Yet, Jesus being part of the Godhead endorsed benefits of the Sun in Ecclesiastes 7:11 and 11:7!

As did John the Baptist and I submit to you both were Sun gazing in conjunction with a biological and mental algorithm to facilitate change in the human body. Not long ago modern humanity scoffed at John the Baptist's desert diet of locust and honey. Modern science now understands locusts contain high levels of chemicals known as phytosterols could control heart-related diseases. Honey is now considered a "super" food because of an array of benefits for the human body. (DUBOIS, 2017)

Ancient man was far ahead of the curve in understanding survival in desert conditions. We can also assume the Sun played a major role in their spiritual transformation. Science has made the connection with Sun and the hormone vitamin D (Holick, 2013) in the human body. Science is slowly making the connection between the human body's endocrine system, which can be normalized by different color spectrums of ultraviolet radiation from the Sun.

The Sun has a greater role in human development which I believe is a component of spiritual transformation. Ancient civilizations would not have left so many artifacts showing us the formula in stone. Many pundits will continue to perpetuate Renaissance paintings with the solar disc behind the head of ancient spiritual characters as sole symbols of Divinity, but the Sun is prominently displayed above spiritual characters, in many other paintings. It is as if the solar secret was memorialized in plain view and after centuries, no longer questioned.

I believe the Pharisees were guilty of the spiritual crime of omission. Jesus was set apart from all other men with His miracles He performed and taught to His Disciples. Even though John the Baptist did not perform miracles, but he did demonstrate precognitive abilities with his accurate predictions of the coming of Jesus. John 10:41 - *And many resorted unto him, and said, John, did no miracle: but all things that John spake of this man were true.*

This lends credence to, Ecclesiastes 7:11, "*Wisdom is good with an inheritance: and by it, there is profit to them that see the sun.*" John the Baptist had preordained knowledge royalty would arrive in human form to reeducate humanity on its complete nature. Over the years I had many spirited debates on why there were no contemporary accounts of the life of Jesus. My response is: Why would there be?

The Roman Empire did not believe Jesus was the Son of God. There goes any mainstream promotion of His life. The Pharisees were part of the Sanhedrin which was a quasi-religious political organization, and they claimed Jesus was a liar. Many critics claim the Bible was written 75 years after the death of Jesus and John died on the island of Patmos in 100 AD. This means oral history was being dispensed by an eyewitness more than 60 years after the resurrection of Jesus, through Spirit.

The teachings of Jesus were most likely practiced and spread across the Earth. I believe the Dark Ages is when these ancient teachings of Jesus were eradicated by the Vatican. There was a concerted effort to break all communication with the Heavenly Kingdom. Did Pope Innocent III, attempt genocide in Southern France because they were a community of Christian Sungazers?

Why would Pope Innocent III pay mercenaries known as Crusaders to murder men, women, and children? This must be when the ancient practice Jesus taught was shared by Mary Magdalene. It makes sense how teachings in Jerusalem made it to the shores of Southern France. The entire country side became spiritually transformed and even in death found bliss.

The objective was and is to keep humanity trapped in the material world. Was this the objective of the Luciferian order to prove humanity could live without Spirit and prosper? How is that working out for the Earth now? The 23rd Psalm speaks of a rod and a staff that provides comfort, yet there are no inquiries as to how they do this? There are so many unanswered questions because the answers were willfully hidden by the largest religious institution, the Vatican.

The ancient Egyptians lasted for almost 30 centuries—from its unification around 3100 B.C. to its conquest by Alexander the Great in 332 B.C., and ancient Egypt was the preeminent civilization in the Mediterranean world. Ancient Egypt lasted for 3,000 years while America is only 242 years old! The ancient Egyptian civilization built upon spiritual cultivation, and Christianity was born on the banks of the Nile. The hieroglyphs and bas-relief walls illustrate they were more than just physical beings with an obsession with death.

I think early European scholars made erroneous assumptions because ancient Egyptians were traveling in the spirit realm *before* the death state. This allowed the ancient Egyptians to receive knowledge from their ancestors. This is no different than Corinthians 12:2, where Paul stated, "*I knew a man in Christ above fourteen years ago, (whether in the body, I cannot tell; or whether out of the body, I cannot tell: God knoweth;) such a one caught up to the third heaven.*" It surely proves where even the Bible states, men could travel to the Heavenly Kingdom while living on the Earth.

This is exactly what the ancient Egyptians were practicing, and their unparallel architecture reflects this knowledge. The Sun, interwoven into the tapestry of their cultural, spiritual practices, and the writing is literally on the walls. The ancient Egyptian *barque* looks remarkably familiar to what modern quantum physicist call wormholes. I believe the ancient Egyptians would travel in spirit form through these wormholes.

We are living in darkness based on the duality of the Heavenly design. When people cross over in Spirit the first thing, every near-death-experience report is a bright white light tunnel. I think it is wonderful 2 Corinthians 12:2 states exactly what the ancient Egyptians were able to do. The rod and staff are prominent features on bas-relief walls and hieroglyphics because they were utilitarian spiritual transformation tools.

It is here we can see a connection to the 23rd Psalm and Sun gazing with the rod and staff. These tools help chemically alter you to feel great peace, comfort, and happiness. Imagine a civilization that collectively practiced Sun gazing with the rod and staff? It must have been very peaceful before it broke.

In closing, we as a people can test these ancient practices for our spiritual transformation. Holy men became Holy by purifying themselves to receive a solar gift that transformed their DNA. These Holy men and women followed a strict program in sequence, which involved baptism by water, prayer, meditation, fasting, purification, and Sun gazing. As these Holy men and women matured through this process, they reached a tipping point and were no longer perceived as just human.

One day the Sun shoots out a solar dove into their bodies and from that moment on they were forever transformed. The copper ankh and was-scepter are necessary to course a subtle current through the melanated skin. Over time you will condition your endocrine system with ultraviolet radiation, while the largest organ in the human body, the skin, is conducting electromagnetic energy. Once the pineal gland is reclaimed it will be repurposed for activating your "tree of life."

You will raise your signal to the height of developing the senses for Spirit. We are spiritual beings first, and we were born into a material prison. I cannot stress enough to seek medical evaluation before you accept this path. It is a radical departure from what our bodies are conditioned and safety first!

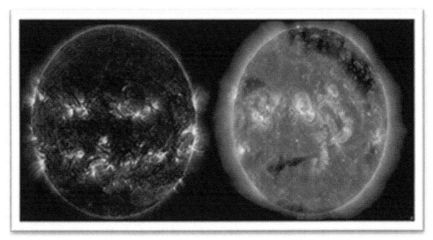

SOHO satellite images of a face on the Sun

When you are medically cleared order a copper ankh and was-scepter. Furthermore, when you are ready to fast, purchase the recommended products for safe fasting. I also recommend you start a Sungazing journal and prepare your prayers for meditation while you Sungaze. Check back with RevelationNow.net as we test low voltage ankhs and stay the course. As some people mature in their Sungazing journey, some have claimed to see a "face" on the Sun.

Some have claimed this face is interactive and it blinks and smiles. Of course, I was shocked to hear this, so I checked with NASA's SOHO satellite and lo and behold, I found a picture of eyes and a mouth on the Sun's surface! Others have claimed the Sun communicates telepathically with them as well. This is now your journey and yours alone.

You are now given pieces of an ancient puzzle, and your discipline will reward with the Holy Spirit. Find a peaceful park or beach to Sun gaze and follow the ancient examples. You will be guided internally during this amazing journey. How exciting is that? Best wishes and may the Lord guide your journey. Peace be with you all and let's light up the world!

Bibliography

Albertus B. Mostert, B. J. (2012, May 21). *PNAS*. Retrieved from Proceedings of the National Academy of Sciences of the United States of America: http://www.pnas.org/content/early/2012/05/16/1119948109

Arbor vitae (anatomy). (2005, December 15). Retrieved from Wikipedia: https://en.wikipedia.org/wiki/Arbor_vitae_(anatomy)

Arnold, L. (2014, November 23). *How Sound Affects You: Cymatics, An Emerging Science*. Retrieved from Ask Audio: https://ask.audio/articles/how-sound-affects-you-cymatics-an-emerging-science

Biello, D. (2009, August 31). *How Sunlight Controls Climate - New computer models begin to suggest how changes in the sun's strength might change weather patterns*. Retrieved from Scientific American: https://www.scientificamerican.com/article/how-sunlight-can-control-climate/

Britannica, T. E. (2016, January 21). *Ashur MESOPOTAMIAN DEITY*. Retrieved from Encyclopædia Britannica: https://www.britannica.com/topic/Ashur-Mesopotamian-deity

Budge, T. b. (1240 BC). *Papyrus of Ani; Egyptian Book of the Dead [Budge]*. Retrieved from UNIVERSITY OF PENNSYLVANIA - AFRICAN STUDIES CENTER: http://www.africa.upenn.edu/Books/Papyrus_Ani.html

C. H. Culp, D. E. (2008, Septemeber 2). *Threshold switching in melanin*. Retrieved from https://aip.scitation.org: https://aip.scitation.org/doi/abs/10.1063/1.322094?journalCode=jap

Catholic Church art. (2018, July 7). Retrieved from Wikipedia: https://en.wikipedia.org/wiki/Catholic_Church_art

Cincinnati, U. o. (2014, March 4). *Range of electrical frequencies that help heal chronic wounds tested by researchers*. Retrieved from ScienceDaily.com: https://www.sciencedaily.com/releases/2014/03/140304113538.htm

Council, M. A. (2009, August 20). *Mayan Calendar Prophecy - The World Will Not End*. Retrieved from Manataka Org.: https://www.manataka.org/page1578.html

Davis, N. (2016, November 3). *Age of onset for multiple sclerosis 'linked to distance from equator'*. Retrieved from The Guardian: https://www.theguardian.com/society/2016/nov/03/age-of-onset-for-multiple-sclerosis-linked-to-distance-from-equator

Denis, D. S. (2001, March 6). *Souled Out*. Retrieved from souledout.org: http://www.souledout.org/cosmology/cossynthreflects/sirius.html

Department of Anatomy, U. o. (1989, July 4). *Cerebrospinal fluid-contacting area of the deep pineal: effects of photoperiod*. Retrieved from US National Library of Medicine National Institutes of Health: https://www.ncbi.nlm.nih.gov/pubmed/2600761

DUBOIS, S. (2017, October 3). *The Nutritional Value of Locusts*. Retrieved from Livestrong Logo: https://www.livestrong.com/article/549444-the-nutritional-value-of-locusts/

Emery., M. (2015). *Double Helical Magnetic Interaction*. Retrieved from leedskalnin.com: http://www.leedskalnin.com/

Gadala, A. (2012, July 24). *Sunlight protects against cancer of the pancreas*. Retrieved from Brain Strom: http://brainstrom.org/sunlight-protects-against-cancer-of-the-pancreas/

Giri, S. N. (2018). *The Christ of India: The Story of Original Christianity*. Cedar Crest: Light of the Spirit Press.

HAGERTY, B. B. (2009, May 20). *Prayer May Reshape Your Brain ... And Your Reality*. Retrieved from NPR.org: https://www.npr.org/templates/story/story.php?storyId=104310443

Half, J. (2017, December 15). *Light therapy and hypothyroidism*. Retrieved from Redlightman.com: https://redlightman.com/blog/red-light-therapy-shown-to-cure-hypothyroidism/

Halo (religious iconography). (2007, April 23). Retrieved from
  Wikipedia:
  https://en.wikipedia.org/wiki/Halo_(religious_iconography)
Harper, J. J. (2009, 7 29). *Suns of God: The Orion Revelation.*
  Retrieved from Reality Sandwhich:
  http://realitysandwich.com/23542/suns_god_orion_revelation/
Hergenrather, J. (2010, October 15). *Linen – The Preferred Fabric for
  Clothing of Healing, Healthy Living and Well Being.*
  Retrieved from Fabrics-Store.com: https://blog.fabrics-
  store.com/2009/05/20/linen-the-preferred-fabric-for-clothing-
  of-healing-healthy-living-and-well-being/
Herschel, W. (2003). *The Hidden Records I*. thehiddenrecords.com.
Holick, M. W. (2013, January 1). *Sunlight and Vitamin D.* Retrieved
  from US National Library of Medicine National Institutes of
  Health:
  https://www.ncbi.nlm.nih.gov/pmc/articles/PMC3897598/
Jaroslav Jan Pelikan, M. E. (n.d.). *Encyclapedia Brittanica*. Retrieved
  from Encyclapedia Brittanica :
  https://www.britannica.com/topic/Roman-Catholicism/The-
  age-of-Reformation-and-Counter-Reformation
Lam, D. (2014, August 5). *The Very Real Benefits of Sunshine for
  Health.* Retrieved from DrLam.com:
  https://www.drlam.com/blog/sunshine-for-health/4891/
Lambdin, T. b. (1998, December 3). *The Nag Hammadi Library - The
  Gospel of Thomas.* Retrieved from The Gnostic Society
  Library: http://gnosis.org/naghamm/gthlamb.html
Laura. (2011, November 25). *The throne of God in the Orion Nebula?*
  Retrieved from ExoTheology & Space-Age Interpretations of
  the Bible:
  https://kitesintheempyrean.wordpress.com/2011/11/25/the-
  throne-of-god-in-the-orion-nebula/
Lavino, A. (2007, March 8). *Mary Called Magdalene.* Retrieved from
  SacredMysteryTours.com:
  http://www.sacredmysterytours.com/mary-
  magdalene/#sthash.8lKB4c57.dpbs
Lazaro, E. d. (2012, June 29). *Melanin as New Material for
  Bioelectronics.* Retrieved from sci-news.com: http://www.sci-
  news.com/biology/article00430.html

Leloup, J.-Y. (2002). *The Gospel of Mary Magdalene*. Rochester: Inner Traditions International.

Life, Water, The Sun, Frequency, and Flower of Life. (2016, April 12). Retrieved from Palmi: http://palmieinarsson.blogspot.com/2013/09/life-water-sun-frequency-and-flower-of.html?view=sidebar

Linsley, A. C. (2012, December 8). *The Horite Ancestry of Jesus Christ*. Retrieved from JUST GENESIS through the lens of Anthropology: https://jandyongenesis.blogspot.com/2012/08/the-horite-ancestry-of-jesus-christ_8.html?m=1

Lloyd, A. B. (1750). Herodotus. In A. B. Lloyd, *Herodotus, Book 2: Commentary 99-182 (Etudes Preliminaires Aux Religions Orientales Dans L'empire Romain, Vol. 43) (v. 3) by A B Lloyd (1997-08-01)* (p. 22). Brill Academic Publishers.

M.D., A. N. (2010). *How God Changes Your Brain: Breakthrough Findings from a Leading Neuroscientist*. New York: United States of Ballantine Books.

Macchi MM, B. J. (2004, Sep-Dec 25). *Human pineal physiology and functional significance of melatonin*. Retrieved from US National Library of Medicine National Institutes of Health: https://www.ncbi.nlm.nih.gov/pubmed/15589268

Maffetone, D. P. (2015, April 29). *Sunlight: Good For the Eyes as well as the Brain*. Retrieved from Dr. Phil Maffetone: https://philmaffetone.com/sun-and-brain/

Maffetone, P. (2012). *The Big Book of Health and Fitness: A Practical Guide to Diet, Exercise*. New York: Skyhorse Publishing, Inc.

Marshall, J. (2014, September 15). *The impact of solar flares on the human mood and psyche*. Retrieved from commdiginews.com: https://www.commdiginews.com/health-science/health/the-impact-of-solar-flares-on-the-human-mood-and-psyche-25963/

Mary Neal, M. (2017, Septemeber 28). *I Got A Glimpse Of Heaven Thanks To A Near-Death Experience. Here's What You Need To Know*. Retrieved from Mind Body Green: https://www.mindbodygreen.com/articles/what-i-learned-about-heaven-from-a-near-death-experience

McClure, B. (2018, January 23). *Orion Nebula is a place where new stars are being born.* Retrieved from Earth Sky: http://earthsky.org/clusters-nebulae-galaxies/orion-nebula-jewel-in-orions-sword

Mead, M. N. (2008, April 11). *Benefits of Sunlight: A Bright Spot for Human Health.* Retrieved from US National Library of Medicine - National Institutes of Health: https://www.ncbi.nlm.nih.gov/pmc/articles/PMC2290997/

Meditation and the Old Testament. (2013, July 6). Retrieved from Eco Insititute : https://eocinstitute.org/meditation/meditation-and-jesus-what-was-their-relationship/

Meyerhoff, D. D. (2000). *Smith College Museum and Ancient Inventions.* Retrieved from Smith.edu: https://en.wikipedia.org/wiki/Baghdad_Battery

Ogden Goelet (Translator), R. F. (2015). The Egyptian Book of the Dead. In R. F. Ogden Goelet (Translator), *The Egyptian Book of the Dead: The Book of Going Forth by Day: The Complete Papyrus of Ani Featuring Integrated Text and Full-Color Images* (p. 192). Chronicle Books LLC.

Orenstein, D. (2011, November 3). *Skin 'sees' UV light, starts producing pigment.* Retrieved from Brown University: https://news.brown.edu/articles/2011/11/melanin

Owens, L. S. (1998, December 1). *The Gospel According to Mary Magdalene.* Retrieved from The Gnostic Society Library: http://gnosis.org/library/marygosp.htm

Perlman, H. (2016, December 2). *The water in you.* Retrieved from The USGS Water Science School: https://water.usgs.gov/edu/propertyyou.html

PINKSTONE, J. (2018, February 7). *Increased UV rays caused by the depletion of the ozone layer could STERILISE trees, warn scientists.* Retrieved from Daily Mail CO UK: http://www.dailymail.co.uk/sciencetech/article-5359141/UV-radiation-cause-plants-sterile.html

Purdin, W. (2014, 2 15). *Secret Mysteries of the Sun Revealed.* Retrieved from New Dawn Magazine: https://www.newdawnmagazine.com/articles/secret-mysteries-of-the-sun-revealed

Purdon, W. (2016, September 20). *Secret Mysteries Of The Sun Revealed*. Retrieved from Truth Theory: https://truththeory.com/2016/09/20/secret-mysteries-sun-revealed/

Putney, A. (2014, May 24). *Resonance in the Essene Gospel of Peace*. Retrieved from Human-Resonance.org : http://www.human-resonance.org/holy_stream.html

RELIGIOUS SUNGAZING. (n.d.). Retrieved from sunlight.xhost.ro/history_of_sun_gazing.htm: http://sunlight.xhost.ro/history_of_sun_gazing.htm

Robert Labensart, C. C. (2016, July 23). *Effortless Breathing- Change your brainwaves – Alpha Theta Breathing*. Retrieved from Therapies for Living: https://therapiesforliving.com/2013/09/effortless-breathing-change-your-brainwaves-robert-labensart-cht-cmt-ryt-santa-rosa-petaluma-corte-madera/

Robertson, Campbell. (2009, July 13). *Iraq Suffers As The Euphrates Dwindles*. Retrieved from The New York Times: https://www.nytimes.com/2009/07/14/world/middleeast/14euphrates.html

Romac, L. P. (1989, September 20). *DNA base sequence changes induced by ultraviolet light mutagenesis of a gene on a chromosome in Chinese hamster ovary cells*. Retrieved from US National Library of Medicine National Institutes of Health: https://www.ncbi.nlm.nih.gov/pubmed/2685319

Rowland, I. D. (2002). *Fathom Archive*. Retrieved from Fathom Archive: http://fathom.lib.uchicago.edu/1/777777122590/

Sample, I. (2016, November 16). *US military successfully tests electrical brain stimulation to enhance mental skills*. Retrieved from The Guardian: https://www.theguardian.com/science/2016/nov/07/us-military-successfully-tests-electrical-brain-stimulation-to-enhance-staff-skills

Santini, S. (2010, August 2). *The Golden Gates*. Retrieved from musterion8.com: http://www.musterion8.com/galacticalignmentandchrist/aug2gates.html

Sarcophagus with Scenes from the Passion of Christ (probably from the Catacomb of Domitilla): Cross with Chi-Rho, laurel wreath, and guards at the tomb, detail of 3rd [C.] panel, mid-4th century A.D. (1989, June 1). Retrieved from Art Images for College Teaching: https://quod.lib.umich.edu/a/aict/x-ec034/EC000_IMG0034?lasttype=boolean;lastview=thumbnail;med=1;resnum=1570;size=20;sort=aict_ti;start=1561;subview=detail;view=entry;rgn1=ic_all;q1=aict

Sarfati, J. (2007, March). *Electric DNA.* Retrieved from Creation.com: https://creation.com/electric-dna

Sayer Ji, F. (2012, March 19). *Race, Skin & Converting Sunlight Into Metabolic Energy.* Retrieved from Green Med Info: http://www.greenmedinfo.com/blog/race-skin-converting-sunlight-metabolic-energy

Simon, S. (2015, June 5). *Melanoma Skin Cancer Rates are on the Rise.* Retrieved from Cancer Org: https://www.cancer.org/latest-news/melanoma-skin-cancer-rates-are-on-the-rise.html

Staff. (2011, September 2). *DISCOVERScientist Proves DNA Can Be Reprogrammed by Words and Frequencies.* Retrieved from Collective Evolution: https://www.collective-evolution.com/2011/09/02/scientist-prove-dna-can-be-reprogrammed-by-words-and-frequencies/

Staff, I. C. (2017, September 25). *Apocalypse Prophecies: Native End of the World Teachings.* Retrieved from Indian Country Today: https://newsmaven.io/indiancountrytoday/archive/apocalypse-prophecies-native-end-of-the-world-teachings-0e7zoaMJEUmdP1z2ln0p9Q/

Staff, N. (2014, 10 18). *The Man Who Coined 'Genocide' Spent His Life Trying To Stop It.* Retrieved from National Public Radio, Inc.: https://www.npr.org/2014/10/18/356423580/the-man-who-coined-genocide-spent-his-life-trying-to-stop-it

Strassman, R. (2000). *DMT: The Spirit Molecule: A Doctor's Revolutionary Research into the Biology of Near-Death and Mystical Experiences.* Rochester: Park Street Press.

Temple, R. (1998). *The Sirius Mystery: New Scientific Evidence of Alien Contact 5,000 Years Ago.* New York: Destiny Books.

Vijayender Bhalla, R. P. (2003, May 4). *DNA electronics*. Retrieved from US National Library of Medicine National Institutes of Health: https://www.ncbi.nlm.nih.gov/pmc/articles/PMC1319189/

Walia, A. (2015, December 11). *Neuroscientist Shows What Fasting Does To Your Brain & Why Big Pharma Won't Study It.* Retrieved from Collective Evolution: https://www.collective-evolution.com/2015/12/11/neuroscientist-shows-what-fasting-does-to-your-brain-why-big-pharma-wont-study-it/

Wall, M. (2013, August 12). *What Causes the Sun's Magnetic Field Flip?* Retrieved from Space.com: https://www.space.com/22310-sun-magnetic-field-flip-mystery.html

What is DNA Activation? (2013, October 14). Retrieved from dnaperfection.com: http://dnaperfection.com/what-is-dna-activation/

Wilson, C. (2017, April 25). *Hungry stomach hormone promotes growth of new brain cells*. Retrieved from New Scientist: https://www.newscientist.com/article/2128695-hungry-stomach-hormone-promotes-growth-of-new-brain-cells/

Wilten, D. A. (2012). *Orion in the Vatican*. Retrieved from Orion in the Vatican: http://www.orioninthevatican.com

Wu, S. (2014, June 5). *Fasting triggers stem cell regeneration of damaged, old immune system*. Retrieved from USC News - University of Southern California: https://news.usc.edu/63669/fasting-triggers-stem-cell-regeneration-of-damaged-old-immune-system/

Yogi, S. (2008, 12 15). *Ancient texts in India say Jesus Christ was a sun gazer*. Retrieved from Sunlightenment.com: sunlightenment.com/ancient-texts-in-india-say-jesus-christ-was-a-sun-gazer/comment-page-1/

Zaidi, A. (2011, January 16). *40-days-its-physiological-psychological-and-spiritual-significance-day-35/*. Retrieved from 40 Day Detox: http://www.40daydetox.com/40-days-its-physiological-psychological-and-spiritual-significance-day-35/